CHURCH, COMMUNITY, AND STATE IN RELATION TO EDUCATION

THE CHURCHES SURVEY THEIR TASK: The Report of the Conference at Oxford, July 1937, on Church, Community, and State

by Sir Walter Moberly, Professor Max Huber, John Maud, President Henry Sloane Coffin, President John Mackay, and with an introduction by J. H. Oldham

1. THE CHURCH AND ITS FUNCTION IN SOCIETY

by Dr. W. A. Visser 't Hooft and Dr. J. H. Oldham   8s. 6d. net

"Challenging and arresting, and will shake us all out of our complacency if we can but see in it a call of God . . . I therefore urge everyone to secure and to read this volume."
—*Church of England Newspaper*

2. THE CHRISTIAN UNDERSTANDING OF MAN

by Prof. T. E. Jessop, Prof. R. L. Calhoun, Prof. N. N. Alexeiev, Prof. Emil Brunner, Pastor Pierre Maury, the Rev. Austin Farrer, Prof. W. M. Horton

3. THE KINGDOM OF GOD AND HISTORY

by Prof. C. H. Dodd, Dr. Edwyn Bevan, Dr. Christopher Dawson, Prof. Eugene Lyman, Prof. Paul Tillich, Prof. H. Wendland, Prof. H. G. Wood

4. THE CHRISTIAN FAITH AND THE COMMON LIFE

by Nils Ehrenström, Prof. M. Dibelius, Prof. John Bennett, The Archbishop of York, Prof. Reinhold Niebuhr, Prof. H. H. Farmer, Dr. W. Wiesner

5. CHURCH AND COMMUNITY

by Prof. E. E. Aubrey, Prof. E. Barker, Dr. Björkquist, Dr. H. Lilje, Prof. S. Zankov, Dr. Paul Douglass, Prof. K. S. Latourette, M. Boegner

6. CHURCH, COMMUNITY, AND STATE IN RELATION TO EDUCATION

by Prof. F. Clarke, Dr. Paul Monroe, Prof. W. Zenkovsky, C. R. Morris, J. W. D. Smith, "X," Prof. Ph. Kohnstamm, J. H. Oldham

7. THE UNIVERSAL CHURCH AND THE WORLD OF NATIONS

by the Marquess of Lothian, Sir Alfred Zimmern, Dr. O. von der Gablentz, John Foster Dulles, Prof. Max Huber, Pastor W. Menn, the Rev. V. A. Demant, Prof. Otto Piper, Canon C. E. Raven

CHURCH, COMMUNITY, AND STATE IN RELATION TO EDUCATION

by

FRED CLARKE

W. ZENKOVSKY

PAUL MONROE

CHARLES R. MORRIS

J. W. D. SMITH

PH. KOHNSTAMM

"X"

J. H. OLDHAM

LONDON

GEORGE ALLEN & UNWIN LTD

MUSEUM STREET

FIRST PUBLISHED IN 1938

vol VI

CONTENTS

(AD41F)

GENERAL INTRODUCTION

FEW will question the significance of the issues which engaged the attention of the conference on Church, Community, and State held at Oxford in July 1937. More important than the conference itself is the continuing process, in which the conference was not more than an incident, of an attempt on the part of the Christian Churches collectively—without, up to the present, the official participation of the Church of Rome, but not without the unofficial help of some of its thinkers and scholars[1]—to understand the true nature of the vital conflict between the Christian faith and the secular and pagan tendencies of our time, and to see more clearly the responsibilities of the Church in relation to the struggle. What is at stake is the future of Christianity. The Christian foundations of western civilization have in some places been swept away and are everywhere being undermined. The struggle to-day concerns those common assumptions regarding the meaning of life without which, in some form, no society can cohere. These vast issues are focussed in the relation of the Church to the State and to the community, because the non-Christian forces of to-day are tending more and more to find embodiment in an all-powerful state, committed to a particular philosophy of life and seeking to organize the whole of life in accordance with a particular doctrine of the end of man's existence, and in an all-embracing community life which claims to be at once the source and the goal of all human activities: a State, that is to say, which aims at being also a Church.

[1] A volume of papers by Roman Catholic writers dealing with subjects closely akin to the Oxford Conference and stimulated in part by the preparatory work for Oxford will be published shortly under the title *Die Kirche Christi: ihre heilende, gestaltende und ordnende Kraft für den Menschen und seine Welt.*

To aid in the understanding of these issues the attempt was made in preparation for the conference at Oxford to enlist as many as possible of the ablest minds in different countries in a common effort to think out some of the major questions connected with the theme of the conference. During the three years preceding the conference studies were undertaken wider in their range and more thorough in their methods than any previous effort of a similar kind on the part of the Christian Churches. This was made possible by the fact that the Universal Christian Council for Life and Work, under whose auspices the conference was held, possessed a Department of Research at Geneva with two full-time directors and was also able, in view of the conference, to establish an office in London with two full-time workers and to set up an effective agency for the work of research in America. There was thus provided the means of circulating in mimeographed form (in many instances in three languages) a large number of papers for comment, of carrying on an extensive and continuous correspondence, and of maintaining close personal touch with many leading thinkers and scholars in different countries.

Intensive study over a period of three years was devoted to nine main subjects. The results of this study are embodied in the six volumes to which this general introduction relates and in two others. The plan and contents of each, and most of the papers, were discussed in at least two or three small international conferences or groups. The contributions were circulated in first draft to a number of critics in different countries and comments were received often from as many as thirty or forty persons. Nearly all the papers were revised, and in some instances entirely rewritten, in the light of these criticisms.

Both the range of the contributions and the fact that

the papers have taken their present shape as the result of a wide international interchange of ideas give these books an oecumenical character which marks a new approach to the subjects with which they deal. They thus provide an opportunity such as has hardly existed before for the study in an oecumenical context of some of the grave and pressing problems which to-day concern the Christian Church throughout the world.

The nine subjects to which preparatory study was devoted were the following:

1. The Christian Understanding of Man.
2. The Kingdom of God and History.
3. The Christian Faith and the Common Life.
4. The Church and Its Function in Society.
5. Church and Community.
6. Church and State.
7. Church, Community and State in Relation to the Economic Order.
8. Church, Community and State in Relation to Education.
9. The Universal Church and the World of Nations.

The last six of these subjects were considered at the Oxford Conference, and the reports prepared by the sections into which the conference was divided will be found in the official report of the conference entitled *The Churches Survey Their Task* (Allen and Unwin, 5s.).

A volume on *The Church and its Function in Society*, by Dr. W. A. Visser 't Hooft and Dr. J. H. Oldham (Allen and Unwin, 8s. 6d.), was published prior to the conference.

Three of the volumes in the present series of six have to do with the first three subjects in the list already given. These are fundamental issues which underlie the study of all the other subjects. The titles of these volumes are:

> *The Christian Understanding of Man.*
> *The Kingdom of God and History.*
> *The Christian Faith and the Common Life.*

The remaining three volumes in the series are a contribution to the study of three of the main subjects considered by the Oxford Conference. These are:

> *Church and Community.*
> *Church, Community and State in Relation to Education.*
> *The Universal Church and the World of Nations.*

The subject of Church and State is treated in a book by Mr. Nils Ehrenström, one of the directors of the Research Department. This has been written in the light of discussions in several international conferences and groups and of a wide survey of the relevant literature, and has been published under the title *Christian Faith and the Modern State* (Student Christian Movement, 6s.).

The planning and shaping of the volume is to a large extent the work of the directors of the Research Department, Dr. Hans Schönfeld and Mr. Nils Ehrenström. The editorial work and the preparation of the volumes for the press owes everything to the continuous labour of Miss Olive Wyon, who has also undertaken or revised the numerous translations, and in the final stages to the Rev. E. S. Shillito, who during the last weeks accepted the responsibility of seeing the books through the press. Valuable help and advice was also given throughout the undertaking by Professor H. P. Van Dusen and Professor John Bennett of America.

J. H. OLDHAM

CHAIRMAN OF THE INTERNATIONAL
RESEARCH COMMISSION.

LIST OF CONTRIBUTORS

CLARKE, FRED, M.A.

Professor of Education in the University of London and Director of the University of London Institute of Education. Formerly Professor of Education at the University of Capetown and at McGill University, Montreal.

Publications: Essays in the Politics of Education; Foundations of History Teaching; A Study of the English Philosophy of Education in 1929 Year Book of International Institute of Teachers College, New York.

ZENKOVSKY, W.

Professor of Philosophy, Psychology, and Pedagogy at the Russian Theological Institute, Paris. Formerly Professor of Philosophy in the University of Kiev, Professor of Psychology in the University of Belgrade, Professor of Psychology in the University of Prague.

Publications: The Problem of Psychical Causality (1915); Psychology of Childhood (1922); The Question of Education in the Light of Christian Anthropology (1934); Various articles in foreign and Russian reviews.

MONROE, PAUL, B.S., Ph.D., LL.D., Litt.D.

Barnard Professor of Education, Columbia University. Director of International Institute of Teachers College. Formerly Director of School of Education, Teachers College, Columbia.

Publications: Source Book in the History of Education for Greek and Roman Period; Thomas Platter and the Educational Renaissance of the Sixteenth Century; Test Book in History of Education; Principles of Secondary Education; China—a Nation in Evolution.

MORRIS, CHARLES RICHARD, M.A.

Fellow, Tutor, and Jowett Lecturer in Philosophy, Balliol College, Oxford.

Publications: Locke, Berkeley, Hume; Idealistic Logic; with J. S. Fulton: In Defence of Democracy.

SMITH, JAMES WALTER DICKSON, M.A.

Formerly Assistant Lecturer in Education, Glasgow University; General Secretary, Scottish Sunday School Union for Christian Education and General Secretary, United Council for Missionary Education.

Publications: Psychology and Religion in Early Childhood.

KOHNSTAMM, Ph., D.Sc.

Professor of Education in Amsterdam and Utrecht and Director of the Institute of Education at the University of Amsterdam. Formerly Professor of Thermodynamics and Lecturer in Philosophy in the University of Amsterdam.
Publications: Schepper en Schepping.

OLDHAM, Joseph Houldsworth, M.A., D.D.

Secretary of the International Missionary Council and Chairman of the International Commission on Research of the Universal Christian Council for Life and Work. Formerly Secretary of the Continuation Committee of the World Missionary Conference.
Publications: The Teaching of Jesus; Christianity and the Race Problem; White and Black in Africa; The Remaking of Man in Africa; with Dr. Visser 't Hooft: The Church and its Function in Society.

TRANSLATORS

Professor Kohnstamm's paper was translated by the Rev. E. L. Allen, and the paper by "X" was translated by Miss L. Goodfellow.

PART I

THE CRISIS IN EDUCATION

by

FRED CLARKE

THE CRISIS IN EDUCATION

A THEORY of education, whatever degree of universal
validity it may claim, will, of necessity, be very largely
determined in the form it assumes by the norms and values
which are dominant in the society from which it takes its
rise. This is true even of theories which have the character
of a protest against certain current norms and values, and
so give sharp expression to that conflict of criteria which
is always present in a living and growing society. Rousseau
is a voice from eighteenth-century France just as Plato
is a voice from the Athens of the fourth century B.C. To
say this is not to deny, or even to detract from, the universal validity of the doctrines that these writers enunciate.
It is rather to suggest that the full significance of what
they have to say can be grasped only when the conditions
of its historical setting are understood and allowance is
made for them.

A similar regard for historical determination is necessary in the field of educational practice also. The relation
between educational effort and social change is misunderstood wherever it is assumed, in somewhat naïve
fashion, that social change is, as it were, the result of a
deliberately planned educational campaign. In recent
years organized efforts of propaganda, whether in the
interests of advertisement or of political parties, have
given some colour to this idea and have tended, in
some quarters, to infect rather seriously the notion of
education itself. But the truth is that practice, in the
organized deliberate sense, arises out of and follows
social change rather than precedes it. In a much more
profound and subtle sense social change *is* contributed to
by education. But not by a species of aggressive propaganda, working against the grain as it were, and calling
itself education.

These considerations will be discussed more fully later. They are mentioned here only to call attention to the aspect of *relativity* which is present in all educational thought and practice. It is particularly necessary to stress this aspect in an age when conflict of norms and values has once more become acute. Issues are apt to be falsely stated and confusion is introduced into the debate if each contributor does not make himself fully aware of the influences which have shaped his own outlook. The writer therefore feels it necessary in the interests of clarity to indicate briefly the influences which, so far as he is aware, have played their part in his case.

The effort to achieve such self-awareness is, for him, mainly one of estimating the part played by English practice and English tradition in determining his thought about education. It is from that source, no doubt, that he derives the conception of freely creative personality as both defining the goal towards which all true education strives and as indicating the nature of the media in and through which it works.

A concept so comprehensive, and, in a sense, so un-compromising, must take a central place in this discussion, so, for the moment, we reserve further discussion of it. Here it will be enough to indicate some more particular attitudes and presuppositions present in the writer's thought and traceable, he believes, to English experience.[1]

First may be noted the presupposition of a sufficient degree of unity in the common life and continuing traditions of a people to permit of the free action of groups and interests within the community in originating and carrying on educational effort. English education is distinctively national, not in spite of, but because of the fact that the

[1] This is not to deny that other forms of social and cultural experience might also have produced them. The writer is concerned only with their origin for his own thought.

actual provision and administration of means of education is the concern of a great number of bodies and associations; local public bodies, private and semi-private associations, and trusts and foundations in bewildering variety.

The central ministry does not administer the schools and, up to the present, has had no occasion to concert measures of education in order to preserve a threatened national unity. Thus the basis of common agreement is of such long standing and of such strength that what may be called the "defensive" motive is not prominent in English education. So the school is "outside politics" in the sense that there is no overt battle of contending parties for the control of it and no set design in government policy to use it as a defensive instrument. Whether this order of things is likely to continue is a question that need not be raised here. The "defensive" motive is certainly not absent and would assert itself if a real threat to national unity arose. We are concerned here only to note that no such threat has arisen so far.

The writer may be permitted to add that he has had some experience of the operation of what is here called the "defensive" motive in South Africa and in Canada, where there are strong non-British groups which have striven for and secured constitutional guarantees for the maintenance of the necessary conditions of cultural defence by education. The effect on the structure of the school system and on the spirit in which it is worked is most marked in both instances.

As we should expect in such conditions as prevail in England, the school itself has the character of a largely autonomous community. In the first place it produces its distinctive educative effects through its functioning as a *community*. In this respect the newer state secondary schools are following the tradition set by the older "Public schools" and are freely encouraged to do so. The school is a small self-contained state in its maintenance of equal law, and at the same time a real society in its efforts to diversify and enrich a common life with a great variety of forms of educative stimulus and opportunity both within the classroom and without.

In the second place it becomes increasingly autonomous, even at the elementary level, in order that it may acquire and use to the full this community character. It can be autonomous with safety, partly because of the depth and strength of that basis of national unity to which reference has been made, and partly because a supply of teachers is forthcoming to whose hands the exercise of such autonomy can safely be entrusted. Changing needs and conditions tend to increase the active participation of the state, but nothing is more strongly marked in English educational policy than the insistence by the state upon its rôle as a *partner* in the common undertaking rather than as a supreme director, still less as a universal provider.

In such a society, working largely on unspoken under-standings transmitted from generation to generation like the soil itself, and needing to take little explicit note of the workings of the order by which it lives, it is natural that the ideal of free creative personality should establish itself as the form in which the educational goal is conceived. Really the educational order produces a distinctive *type*, adapted to life in the given society just as any other educa-tional order—even the most authoritarian—will do. But the bonds sit so lightly and are so little felt, the traditional social order and the educational order are so much the same thing, that the actual *experience* is one of freedom. Nor is this all illusion. Rather one may hazard the sug-gestion that in the relatively undesigned working out of the English system in peculiarly fortunate circumstances, the essential conditions of substantial freedom have been stumbled upon, as it were. There are the necessary constraint and conditioning for the shaping of a type, and at the same time these operate so unobtrusively and congenially as to safeguard the inner life of the pupil, leaving him to see himself as the artificer of his own personality.

From a standpoint thus determined the very real and acute crisis in which Western education is now involved wears the appearance of a sharp challenge both to the presuppositions upon which such an order as that of England has worked, and to that belief in free personality as the goal of education which has emerged from the working. To say this, however, is to do no more than indicate the *form* that the crisis takes in regard to policy and practical objectives. The deeper *causes* are, no doubt, to be sought in profound changes of attitude towards life and towards values regarded as integral to well-being, which have already had a long history. It is the purpose of other papers to throw light upon these deeper changes, especially as they bear upon the Christian standpoint and the particular form of the concrete obligations which are imposed upon the Christian by the resulting situation. For the purposes of this paper it is proposed to view the actual crisis in education as taking the form indicated above, that of a challenge to the whole idea of free personality as an objective, and of a passionate repudiation of those social and educational forms which have such an objective in view.

Citizens of free societies, such as England, if they are properly aware of the conditioning factors of their own freedom, will need to take some care in defining the difference between themselves and the totalitarians in this regard. That the difference is wide and profound is obvious enough. But can it be fairly defined as one between freedom and discipline taken quite simply? Would the totalitarian agree that he has surrendered the ideal of free personality? Might he not rather argue that he has discovered and given effect to the necessary conditions of it? Conversely, could the English advocate of freedom, for instance, deny that the freedom he seeks in life and education is conditioned by a very real social discipline? The "free" citizen could not deny that the authority of a determinate social and cultural order is essential to any effective education. If he did attempt to deny it his own practice would belie him.

The issue between freedom and discipline stated abstractly is in fact unreal. It would be nearer the truth to say that the difference lies between two conceptions of authority as residing in a given social and political order. The totalitarian would seem to be prepared to take such authority as absolute whatever may be the philosophy or the mystical creed by which he attempts to justify such acceptance.

To the "free" citizen such a proceeding seems to strike at the heart of the very idea of humanity while to the Christian it is the flat negation of all that is most vital in his belief. Neither would deny the reality of social authority in education. What he would most strenuously deny is the claim to absoluteness. Social authority is to both of them in the last resort *contingent*. It may not claim the last obedience. Its purpose, it would be argued, is to educate men to the point where they can catch their own vision of that to which the last obedience is due. Humanist and Christian might differ as to the seat of ultimate authority, but neither would find it in a form of society or in that organization of society for common action which we call the state.

For a clear and authoritative statement of the ideal around which the crisis has arisen we may turn to the most distinguished of modern English writers on the philosophy of education. Sir Percy Nunn in his *Education: Its Data and First Principles*, puts it thus (p. 5):

"We shall stand throughout on the position that nothing good enters into the human world except in and through the free activities of individual men and women, and that educational practice must be shaped to accord with that truth."

And again (p. 10):

"Freedom is, in truth, the condition if not the source of all the higher goods. Apart from it duty has no meaning, self-sacrifice no value, authority no sanction."

Such words can still evoke a passionate response from teachers, and not in England alone, and they state the issue fairly, not denying the value and necessity of duty, self-sacrifice, and authority, but claiming that, without freedom, these things have neither meaning nor validity.

What then has happened to precipitate this crisis in Western education? From the standpoint here taken it may be suggested that as a result, no doubt, of causes that have long been operating, there has taken place since the Great War a widespread breakdown of that settled social and cultural order under which it was possible to carry on the sure and ordered educational process of producing the cultural *type* in such a way as to guarantee free and expansive conditions and to afford a wide range of free variation and creative adventure within the whole. It is suggested, that is, that totalitarian philosophy is a normal *ex post facto* phenomenon, a sort of "rationalizing" if not of social calamity, then of the readiest means to emerge from the consequences. The essential fact is the social and cultural breakdown itself, rather than the philosophy which emerged from the efforts to repair it.

This *emergency* character of totalitarian doctrine needs always to be kept in view.

Where the pre-war conditions of continuity, security, and acceptance still exist in sufficient strength it remains possible:

i. To continue to proclaim the doctrine of free personality as the goal of education and to produce a type which, while being genuinely a *type*, is free to develop further possibilities and so to become increasingly universal—more representatively *human*. For the type is not regarded as wholly fixed or defined beforehand. Nor is the nation taken as absolute. Rather is it the conservator and vehicle of values which, though they assume a distinctive form in that national type, are nevertheless, in principle, universal and so communicable.

ii. To contemplate and maintain what Bergson would call an "open" society, that is, a society which is expecting and welcoming further development of the "type" and ready to assimilate to itself the enrichments which the creative life of free personalities can bring. If, as Nunn argues, nothing good enters the human world in any other way, society is dooming itself to stagnation if it binds strictures around this one source of growth.

One may recall here the dictum of Professor W. E. Hocking that "Education must communicate the type and must provide for growth beyond the type." If the words "growth beyond the type" should seem a little perplexing, and a little out of step with the present argument, perhaps we might substitute "further growth of the type towards the universal."

The national communities in the world in which it is still possible to maintain these attitudes in practice are

now much reduced in number, and may be reduced still
further, for we have witnessed since the war the rise of
powerful state organizations concentrating under their
own control all possible instruments of educational influence and propaganda. It has been left to our age to
make the discovery of the enormous power that modern
invention may place in the hands of a resolute and ruthless
central government. A revolution has taken place in our
time comparable to that which was brought about by
the invention of gunpowder, but on a vaster scale and
with much more subtle consequences. What the earlier
revolution did for feudalism, the later one may do for
democracy, unless the urgency of the situation is grasped
so as to make possible that reorientation which is
demanded.

The command of influence thus concentrated in a few
directing hands is used to produce a sharply defined type,
obedient and acquiescent yet capable of intense energy
and enthusiasm within the set limits. Readiness to accept
the idealized nation group as an absolute (or even a
deity) is usually a central characteristic of the type.
The limits of permissible variation are narrowly drawn
and variation beyond them is disloyalty and punishable
as such.

Personality being thus equated with the sharply
defined type within a fixed social pattern which claims
something of the sanctity of a divine revelation, there is
little room either for the free explorative play of personality
beyond the type, or for that cumulative growth and adaptation of the social whole at its "open" end which such
free play of personality might bring about. For, it would
appear, there is to be no open end. Neither is there any
margin of adventure or penumbra beyond the individual
type, or beyond the existing social order in which fresh
possibilities of enrichment may be sought. All is clear-cut

and patterned, decisive and inclusive. Adventure and creation must take place wholly within it.

Yet it would be flying in the face of clear facts to assert roundly that the thrust and *élan* of creative personality have disappeared altogether from such societies. For the time at least there is too much evidence to the contrary. It is on the basis of such evidence that the totalitarian might argue that, so far from having crushed out creative personality, he has in fact set up the positive conditions for its release and fulfilment. It would be necessary then to join issue with him on the question of *method*, whether by his method of propaganda and dictation he really does produce the result and *can go on producing it*. For only the lapse of time can provide the final answer. It has yet to be shown that the totalitarian system of things will *wear* when conditions are less excited and feverish than they are to-day.

But in order to show that there may, for a time at least, be a real sense of expansion and release, a conviction of passing into "freedom," arising from the acceptance of rigorous discipline in a common enterprise, it is not necessary to turn to the totalitarian countries. The point may be illustrated from the declarations of young Englishmen either in welcoming such an occasion of release, or in expressing a wistful desire for the conditions that would bring it.

The first example is a sonnet by Rupert Brooke, written shortly after the outbreak of the Great War.

> Now God be thanked Who has matched us with His hour
>   And caught our youth, and wakened us from sleeping,
> With hand made sure, clear eye, and sharpened power,
>   To turn, as swimmers, into cleanness leaping.
> Glad from a world grown old and cold and weary,
>   Leave the sick hearts that honour could not move,
> And half-men, and their dirty songs and dreary
>   And all the little emptiness of love!

Oh! we, who have known shame, we have found release there,
Where there's no ill, no grief, but sleep has mending,
Nought broken save this body, lost but breath;
Nothing to shake the laughing heart's long peace there,
But only agony, and that has ending;
And the worst friend and enemy is but Death.

Brooke himself died, a soldier, not long afterwards. Does the sonnet lack the ring of truth, of a glad acceptance of what to him was release and freedom? And if this is the temper and the mood upon which the totalitarian educator plays and this the result he produces, can it be argued that he fails to evoke creative personality? We may well ask, indeed, whether such release may be achieved only at the price of war or threat of war. But that throws upon us the onus of devising a plan of education which will achieve it under conditions of settled peace. And that, in fact, is one aspect of the task with which democratic societies are now faced.

Let us now take another example of generous youth, in this case not finding his release, but bitterly uneasy with the longing for it. In Lord Lytton's deeply suggestive memoir of his son Antony, killed in a flying accident, there is a letter in which Antony says:

"Give them (i.e. the war generation) their due—they were good. But any fool can fight a war: he has to. There is no alternative. It is simple. It is straightforward, and when you are dead you are great. But to live at peace, is difficult, tedious, heartbreaking, complicated, twisty, and uncertain. And when you are dead you are little."

In spite of the difference of circumstance the resemblance to Brooke's sentiment of twenty years earlier is striking enough.

In another letter further light is thrown on the temper

which beyond all question finds reason to chafe at conditions that refuse to afford opportunity for the desired freedom and release. He says:

> "The pacifists have set about me the wrong way. That's all. I admire strength and vitality and clarity of thought, action and expression. And I admire death. I like black and I like white. But not grey."

We do not wish to suggest that such a temper is wholly admirable or that it may not arise from some misdirection in education, but it is present, particularly in high-spirited and generous youth, and may be accentuated by economic stress and the timidities of the crowd. And it is the totalitarian who seems most successful in drawing upon it to-day. However that may be, the widespread existence of such a temper among youth is a factor of no small importance in constituting the crisis with which education now finds itself faced.

When we ask, as we must, what are the forces which have brought about such a general rejection of the social and cultural conditions under which the ideal of free personality, as here understood, can have full play, it must be replied that one of them is certainly insecurity. We mean here not only insecurity in the military sense, or even economic insecurity, itself a powerful factor. We mean also moral and emotional insecurity against aimlessness and despair. The examples quoted show that this may be acutely felt among peoples not living under conditions of severe stress. The phenomenon may perhaps be traced to the operation of disintegrating influences which have been at work upon the European spirit from at least the time of the Renaissance. A regenerated education will have to take account of them, but space does not permit of a discussion here. If, however, one adds to these deep-seated general influences, in the case of a particular

people, national catastrophe, economic stress, a loosening
of the roots of community and widespread and feverish
recourse to heady theories, one can easily understand that
disintegration may proceed so far as to call for violent
measures of rehabilitation by sheer pressure. And we
know now how readily violence can find means of sancti-
fying itself and of propagating the doctrine that appears
to justify it.

But there is also another factor contributing to the
situation. It is a relatively new factor and the totalitarian
has learned how to take account of it and use it. We may
call it Mass Assertion. We mean by the term the active
impulse of men in the mass to refuse any fatalistic submission to circumstance. The decline of older religious
beliefs and ways of life leaves the way open to Promethean
faith in man's collective power to help himself by drastic
"reconstruction." A century or more of popular education
and mechanical progress lend both driving power and
direction to the faith, whether it aims at the refashioning
and reinspiration of an old order or the creation and
maintenance of a new one. Here again the phenomenon
is not confined to the totalitarian lands.

The resulting problem for education in the democracies
is formidable in the extreme. Yet all too little thought has
been given to it in the form in which it now presents itself.
It is not easy to reconcile with the observed facts the
complacent picture so frequently drawn of millions of
sober, well-informed, and serious citizens, studiously
devoting themselves to the task of arriving at sound judgments on each of the vastly complicated problems upon
which a modern government has to make decision. Much
current democratic theory is far too naïvely optimistic
and over-simplified to provide an adequate basis for the
kind of education that a modern democracy needs. In
point of fact we are more often saved by departing from

it than by adhering to it. This is not at all to agree that the democratic order is outmoded. To do so would be to abandon the philosophy of education which has been placed in the forefront of this discussion. It is, however, to suggest that the *technique* of democracy may, in these times, be much more complicated than the nineteenth century realized. If so, there is a task for democratic education not yet fully formulated.

To the fruits of all such tendencies towards forcible collective action the state is legatee. Never was there an engine of such power. Fierce battles for the control of it are to be expected, as are also the ruthless uses made of it by the victors. For increasingly it is identified not only with the nation but with the Church also, even when the Church repudiates the name and becomes a quasi-religious cult of anti-religion. So a situation arises in which states may be described as in war-formation on all fronts simultaneously: economic, religious, intellectual and educational, as well as military.

The description suggests that the condition can hardly be permanent, however fruitful of tragedy it may be while it lasts. Its effects upon education and upon prevailing philosophies of education have already been hinted at. They need not be elaborated here. It is of more concern that the peoples who still continue the free tradition should draw the right conclusion for themselves, and especially that they should enquire how far the totalitarian revolution is the result of universal modern tendencies which are present in greater or less degree in all countries. Then, without surrendering their central faith, they can return to fundamental principles, restating their philosophies and readjusting their practice to meet the inadequacies and weaknesses which the earthquake shocks of recent years have revealed.

To some suggestions towards this end we may now turn.

The first is to call for a more discerning recognition, in some democratic communities at least, of the fact that there can be no effective education, no adequate achievement of personality, apart from the basic discipline of an established social and cultural order. There are doctrines of education which, legitimately enough perhaps in some circumstances, take an established order for granted without elaboration of its bearings. There are others, however, that do not fairly avow the real anarchism by which they appear to be inspired. Either they draw upon a social capital, without acknowledgement—a procedure which is quite possible where the pupils are advantageously placed socially and economically—or, at the worst, they encourage disintegration by an unconditioned cult of "free" personality, which is really a propagation of anarchism. It is in secure and prosperous societies where the illusion of "unconditioned" free personality may most easily arise, but even so it is harmful both to the society and the individual.

The pedagogic problem here is that of discipline in the sense of training a pupil to recognize himself and his own best interests in the requirements of an authority which, at first sight, seems to be imposed from without. From this point of view discipline has a threefold function: (1) To organize and direct the essential process of taking on a culture by an individual, a process which is at the same time a development and enhancement of the individual's own powers; (2) to bring about the "internalizing" of the ruling sanctions and values of the culture so that from being external standards and compulsions they become consciously accepted and applied as personal criteria; (3) to build up the volitional structure so that action may conform to insight.

These assured, the essentials of personality are present. It is not wholly honest to let them come by chance or surreptitiously as it were, under the illusion that the cult of free personality derives wholly from inner impulse. And it is disastrous to educate as though it is immaterial whether these essentials are secured at all.

In the second place education in the free societies may have to take more account of the necessities of an *organic* order in society, when the world of experience has become so complex and the necessities of the common life demand so high a degree of differentiation of function. The interpretation of democratic equality comes into question here. It may be that there are societies in which the postulate is being interpreted altogether too naïvely and crudely, and where too little account is being taken in the working of the educational system of the need for continuous *selection* somewhat in the Platonic manner. As was suggested above, far-reaching changes in democratic technique may have to take place and the principle of differentiation may come to affect political as well as economic functioning. It would be wholly undemocratic if such changes involved any withdrawal of the franchise or any reduced emphasis on the responsibility of every citizen for the common good. But there are many ways in which that responsibility may be discharged. Our ideas of democracy have probably been too exclusively political, and our education has no doubt been affected by this. And in general, so far from aristocracy being opposed to democracy, the future may emphasize the proviso that a democracy which is not organized so as to evolve continuously in its working its own "natural" aristocracy is doomed to futility and possibly worse. Should this be so there is an obvious task for education as well as for political readjustment before us.

More immediately urgent perhaps is a group of questions concerning the proper functions of the state in education. There could hardly be a worse time than the present for any attempt to determine what the functions of the state should be under conditions of normal security and maturity, for we have seen reason to think that the present attitude of men towards the state is abnormal, the result of a fevered and unhealthy condition of society.

Further, it seems probable that differences in degree of administrative direction and control of education by the state cannot safely be taken as measuring accurately degrees of democratic freedom. For profound differences of history and circumstance have to be taken into consideration. In democratic England, a high degree of initiative and large powers of control are left to purely local, or even voluntary, bodies. But in Australia, which is at least equally democratic and almost aggressively "British," local bodies, if they exist at all, have little or no initiative, and popular education is administered under a highly centralized state system which, in form at least, is much nearer to that of France than to that of Britain. It would seem that the citizens of a democracy may, according to circumstance, keep their "rights" in respect of control of education in their own hands and exercise them, as it were, directly, or they may choose to *deposit* these rights with the state as trustee, relying on the use of ordinary political controls to guard against abuse. In some quarters there is a tendency to equate "democratic" with "decentralized" in classifying forms of educational administration by the state. But it is extremely doubtful whether such a tendency has any real justification. The true differentia of a "democratic" education must be sought in another direction, in the region of *intention* and *aim*. Where it is accepted that the real educator is the community, not the state, and that the interest of the community is best served by securing a maximum of opportunity to free personality, the essentials of a democratic order are present. The legal, administrative, regulative organ called the state is then, towards the community, an *agent* and, towards the individual, a *trustee*. It is, on the other hand, when state and community are identified that democratic values in education can no longer have free course and this seems to be the condition now reached in totalitarian countries.

As has been suggested, non-totalitarian communities may make very free use of state action in furthering education. There is, no doubt, a radical incompatibility between the real processes and ends of education and some forms of state action. But in a freely developing community experience is likely to reveal these cases and, conversely, to discover which modes of action are, in its special circumstances, most consonant with genuine educative effect. Thus, while we might expect in general that the healthier and more developed the community the more spontaneous its educating activity will be and the less dependent upon the state, no absolute rule can be laid down—the question is, at bottom, one of the prevailing philosophy of life and education rather than of the administrative forms in which the philosophy seeks expression. The Australian and the Englishman, no doubt, share the same essential philosophy, but how differently they express it in their respective educational systems!

Perhaps we get nearer to the heart of the matter when we return to the conception of free personality as the governing ideal and ask the question: Can the ideal of free personality be consistently held, can it be safely held, except as an article of faith which is essentially religious? By "safely" we mean safely for society and social cohesion. For it would seem, without faith in an ideal whole which both sustains and transcends the free personalities, either anarchy will ensue, or a totalitarian order will slip in as it were, to fill the void left by an absent religion. The prob-

lem which no doctrine of free personality is able to avoid
is the problem of obligation: Why should such individua-
lities cohere in a society and how should they be brought
to cohere? Hobbes could solve the problem only by a
virtual elimination of the free personalities. Rousseau
thought he had solved it in his form of the social contract,
but never quite escapes from a kind of oscillation between
the two poles of complete individual freedom and the
authority of the general will.

May it not be that the democratic ideal of free personality, like that of the closely allied one of equality, is in
the last resort undemonstrable, and must be held as an
article of faith of a universal religion? There is, indeed, a
ground of unity among men afforded by the common life
in time and place, the sharing in a history and a present
common home, which constitute the community and out
of which the state emerges as formulation and guarantee.
Nor does it seem practicable to contemplate the attain-
ment of any larger, more comprehending unity except
by this route, by way of the nation-state. The way to a
league of mankind lies through a league of *nations*.

But experience has shown that freedom of personality
as here conceived is always insecure, even in the most
liberal of states, so long as it is grounded upon and
guaranteed by nothing more abiding and universal than
the laws of a particular state. There are those who fear
for its future even in England. Unless, then, men are aware
of a ground and guarantee of free personality as a supreme
value, deeper and more universal than those which the
state can offer, the fear of anarchy and disintegration will
always be there to limit human possibilities. Out of that
fear may emerge at any time the totalitarian reaction, not
wholly without justification. And, as we have seen, out
of the reaction there may emerge, in due course, a religion
to rationalize and justify it. Violence is sanctified, and

the time actually does come "when whosoever killeth you shall think he doeth God service."

In his *Man and the State*, published ten years ago, Professor Hocking has a prophetic passage which illuminates the principles we are here suggesting. He says:

> "Men are always more widely conscious of the fact of underlying unity than they are of its nature, and in proportion as they lose their grasp of metaphysical reality, they incline to recover their loss by making gods of social groups, of 'society' or 'state' or 'humanity,' to the boundless confusion of political theory, and to vast practical losses in terms of liberty, as will appear in due time."

If, then, the ultimate guarantee of free personality, with all that it means for education, is religious, what will be the character of such a religion? Clearly it must be a religion of love, as an absolute obligation. It must also be a religion which holds out no hope of any earthly achievement of perfection and yet insists upon the striving towards perfection as another absolute obligation. That is, it will recognize "Sin" as the consciousness of this inescapable tension. And it will recognize no final resting-place for men between the City of Swine and the City of God. It will eschew hate, it will look for the sources of evil and of regeneration *within*, and will not succumb to the prevailing externalism and the trick of "projecting" our own sense of guilt upon others so that we may have the satisfaction of "fighting evil" with no disquiet to our own consciences. It will also be sceptical of all earthly Utopias however religious the garb in which they array themselves.

Such a religion looks surprisingly like a revitalized and regenerated Christianity. The suggestion implied here is not merely pragmatic in the manner of "Why not try Christianity?" Still less is it cynical, as though one should say: "If Christianity had not existed it would have been necessary to invent it." Rather is it a suggestion that in Christianity there is conveyed, however darkly and figuratively, profound *knowledge*, knowledge of truth about life, neglect of which can lead only to the dehumanizing of men.[1]

If this is so, the whole problem of what we have been accustomed to call "religious" education takes on a new and tremendous significance. For we are now concerned not with a department or phase of education, but with the whole meaning of education itself, the achievement of freedom by adequate knowledge and recognition of its conditions. And this has to be carried through with full recognition of all that "science" and "civilization" now mean in the lives of men.

In this short paper it is not possible to develop fully all the implications of such a theme. We must content ourselves with a few reflections, having in view the necessities of the practical situation.

In the first place it should be clear that the question at issue involves much more than the relations between Church and state. The Church must, indeed, be "free" within the state, but it must also be ready to subordinate

[1] A word of explanation seems to be called for here. The writer has taken his allotted task to be that of attempting an exposition of the contemporary crisis in education in terms as objective as his own personal experience and outlook would permit. He was not asked to present a characterization of the crisis worked out from a specifically Christian standpoint taken from the outset. (It was understood that provision for studies of this kind would be made elsewhere in the series.)

Hence, tentative conclusions to the effect that ultimate guarantees of freedom among men lie beyond the Law of the State, and are essentially religious in character, and that a religion capable of providing such guarantees will have the typical features of Christianity, must be taken as arising from the argument itself. They must not be read as though they purported to be an adequate and systematic statement of Christian criteria as such.

its interests—or apparent interests—as a *de facto* association, to the supreme end for which it exists. Inhibitions
such as those of the rich young ruler may well be fatal.
In the practical work of education, while Churches will
continue to conduct their own schools so long as they are
permitted to do so, they may find their real task more and
more in spreading through the community at large that
profounder consciousness of the grounds of its unity to
which reference has been made. And this implies not any
attempt to "capture" the state—which long experience
has shown may be only the beginning of virtual apostasy
on the side of the Church and of tyranny for the mass—
nor any energetic propaganda. It implies rather the
exemplification of the Christian life with full regard to the
facts of the modern world. Freedom so to live is the one
demand upon the state which every Christian must make.
The living of such a life must have its inevitable social
consequences; but these will follow from the decisions
and actions of individual Christians striving to realize
in their citizenship the human obligations which their
faith imposes. They will not or should not follow from
the imposition by a Church upon its members of the
obligation to follow a particular line of policy as citizens.
Indeed the whole problem of the political action of
Churches as such seems to have changed its nature now
that the presuppositions upon which it proceeded no
longer hold as they did.

In face of the inescapable facts of the present situation
it is difficult to offer any suggestions, more precise than
those given, about the place of religion and the Church
in education in the kind of society which now appears to
be taking shape. Postulates which were valid enough a
generation or two ago no longer hold, now that Christianity has been so widely rejected and great communities
are now using all the vast powers of the state in order

to reconstruct European society upon a basis quite other than that upon which it has rested for nearly two thousand years. We should not underestimate the immensity of the crisis which is now upon us, or fail to realize that what is at issue is not merely the continuance of this or that Church, or of any particular plan of providing for religious education, but the validity and necessity of the Christian philosophy of life itself. Further light upon these problems of organization and practice must wait upon the decision of that supreme issue.

In conclusion we should wish to re-emphasize the difficulty, even the danger, of arriving at precise formulations about practice in a world so abnormal, and in many respects so provisional. So much is in flux, and we may take leave to doubt whether any of the new crystallizations which have so far emerged have much prospect of permanence in their present form.

It may be enough, therefore, to conclude with some suggestions about the kind of order which those bred in the "free" tradition of life and education would find satisfactory. We should hope that in mature and reasonably secure communities, society itself would be the active educational agent, freely creating schools and other educational means out of its own life and resources in terms of its own varied needs and values. It would use the state only where process of law was required for such ends as the guarantee of opportunity, the provision of means, the securing of minorities, the maintenance of standards, and the protection of the reasonable freedom of the teachers. Not only Churches but other groups would have free course for their educational activities within the law. Limits to toleration there would always have to be, but the ruling consideration in imposing such limits would be the desire to maintain the positive conditions of real freedom. Finally, one would hope for a society which has met and fairly solved, as no society has yet done, that problem of the true nature of *democratic discipline* which is now at the heart of our crisis. In times of good fortune, of security and prosperity, democracies do not care to hear about discipline. So when the crisis comes and a form of discipline is demanded which will serve to meet the crisis without sacrifice of the essentials of freedom, the democracies are unprepared and the advantage shifts to the totalitarians. Then new religions are born from the desire to conquer fear and the hitherto neglected discipline becomes a kind of god who will not hear of freedom. It may be that this is the real problem with which education in the democracies is now squarely faced, to devise educational forms and procedures from which may emerge a discipline whose service is perfect freedom.

The totalitarian revolution may prove to have performed a real service to the democracies if it burns into their consciousnesses that which they have been disposed to forget—that there is no true freedom which is not, in a very real sense, a kind of obedience.

THE TOTALITARIAN IDEA AND THE
PROBLEM OF EDUCATION

by

W. ZENKOVSKY

THE TOTALITARIAN IDEA AND THE
PROBLEM OF EDUCATION

INTRODUCTION

THE totalitarian tendencies of our day—a phrase which denotes a complex of very varied phenomena of the post-war period—were not evoked by any educational problems, nor by any crisis in, or criticism of, contemporary views on education. These totalitarian tendencies are connected with the general crisis in civilization which had been coming to a head for a long time, and which became particularly acute after the war. They are also connected with the present violent and profound disturbances in the realm of politics, in the theory and practice of democracy, and finally, with a new outburst of national self-consciousness. When these totalitarian tendencies first appeared on the scene they had no connection with the sphere of education; yet, in the course of events, possibly no other sphere of life has been more profoundly affected by these tendencies, nor has any other sphere been subjected to such persistent pressure. Totalitarian tendencies have penetrated into education from the outside, but having done so, they have deeply stirred and even revolutionized the most vital forces within the realm of education, have called into being a counter-movement, and in a certain sense have evoked a creative response. We might even say, without fear of exaggeration, that this particular sphere of life provided a specially favourable soil for totalitarian tendencies, for education was passing through a serious internal crisis when it first came into touch with totalitarianism which immediately claimed to be able to solve all the difficulties which had provoked this crisis.

Primarily, and chiefly, totalitarianism is an *ideological*

phenomenon. This does not by any means weaken its intensity and effectiveness in the political sphere, or the reality of its dominion over life—that is, where totalitarianism is able to control the situation. Yet its "creative effort" has been tempered by actual life, and will undergo still further changes, whereas the ideological process of "fermentation" which evoked totalitarianism is penetrating into life more strongly and more profoundly than it seemed to penetrate at first sight. This is especially clear to those who look at contemporary life, at the intellectual and spiritual changes which are taking place in the modern world, "in the light of Christ." It may be that this can be explained by the peculiar position of Christianity in the whole historical process of modern times; in a certain sense it is true to say that it remains aloof from history. Christianity is profoundly connected with the recent past, with all its creative quests, its Utopian idealism, its faith in democracy, its passion for liberty and its "personalistic" sentiment. Yet it neither could nor would identify itself with the past epoch in civilization which inwardly repelled Christianity by its secularism, by its self-sufficient "neutrality" of culture, by the way in which it defaced and distorted the Christian message of the Kingdom of God, by its substitution of Utopia, which establishes justice by force and violence, for the Christian idea of brotherhood. In the "revaluation of values" which takes place in the world to-day and represents the driving force behind the modern crisis in civilization, Christianity not only takes a creative part, as an eternal factor in history, but it faces the task of rebuilding the whole of life on the basis of the Christian idea, and it does so with the consciousness that it is in possession of new energy and of new inspiration. In the light of this it becomes evident that Christianity *is* the true source and the true basis of the true totalitarian conception, which is only revealed

in part in the non-Christian and even anti-Christian
tendencies of this period of transition. This juxtaposition
of forces which are so different and yet are united in the
same conception, both intensifies the relationships and
confuses the whole picture: the totalitarian tendencies
of the non-Christian, and especially of the anti-Christian
type, are persistently seeking for an independent foundation, whether it be in some mythology of "blood and
soil," or in dialectic materialism, or in something else. It
remains true, however, that Christianity, as such, proves to
be a powerful factor—even though it in some cases be a
secret one—in the changes which are taking place in the
civilization of our own day. In this particular instance
the whole strength of Christianity lies in the fact that it
is neither a "party" nor a "tendency," but an eternal
force in history; in short, that it is the Church. All its
external divisions cannot eliminate either its basic or its
historical unity, even if this basic unity be manifested in
the depths and not on the surface of history. The power
of Christianity lies in the fact that it aims at truth and
goodness, and not at external power and success. Christianity, therefore, comprehends and makes a mystical
synthesis of all the truth and goodness produced by the
"stream" of history. The attitude of Christianity to the
whole subject of education, to the crisis towards which
events have so long been moving, to all the creative experiments in this sphere and the sense of a deep inward confusion, has never been *academic*; it has always been living
and creative. The fact that all contemporary totalitarian
movements make such an effort to "capture the heart of
the young"[1] to rebuild the entire system of school and of
extra-mural education, lays a grave obligation upon the
Christian conscience; it is the duty of Christianity to

[1] G. Giese speaks of the "revolution of the heart" (*Staat und
Erziehung*, p. 7. 1933).

come forth at this very moment in history and to enter the realm of education, bringing into it all its truth and authority. It is a Christian duty to throw a clear light upon the nature of the totalitarian tendencies of our day, and to show plainly that the true basis of a new civilization, the true way to create the "new man," is to be found in Christianity alone. All over the world to-day forces are struggling and competing in the effort to capture the soul of youth. Christianity cannot fail to take a very active and vital part in this struggle; *sine ira et studio* to the "old" humanity whose day is passing, and to the "new" humanity which is about to be born, it must show all the eternal truth and the historical vitality and effectiveness of Christianity.

THE TOTALITARIAN IDEA AND TOTALITARIAN TENDENCIES

In order to see clearly both the meaning and the historical significance of totalitarian tendencies (as they are manifested in the crisis in education) we must first of all emphasize an important distinction which will help us to avoid many mistakes which frequently occur in contemporary writings. We must make a clear distinction between the totalitarian "idea" and totalitarian "tendencies," which manifest themselves differently in different countries and are associated with movements which are sharply opposed to one another.

Our present epoch is certainly an epoch of great and universal change; it witnesses many transitional groupings analogous to what chemists call "unstable compounds." The totalitarian tendencies are not an artificial "invention" nor are they a peculiar feature of the present day, a feature which, as it were, has been imposed from without and is therefore alien. Its historical significance lies in the fact that it actually issues from the very depths of history, yet as it would seem to an outside observer, it is indissolubly blended with the "telluric forces"[1] which were set in motion by the upheaval caused by the war. It is quite natural that totalitarian tendencies, which are phenomena wholly ideological in character, should stand out sharply and sometimes even with an intolerable harshness in the political sphere. Here, however, we may also observe a new phenomenon, one which is only partially connected with the totalitarian tendency, and in many respects is even wholly independent of it—I mean the modern glorification of the state, or "étatisme."

"ÉTATISME," OR THE GLORIFICATION OF THE STATE

By "étatisme" we mean that the state assumes functions and rights which are beyond its purely "technical" purposes. The state becomes an absolute; its value is supreme; it is regarded as an ultimate form of "integration"[2] of the scattered forces of history, as an ultimate which has the legal right to control all the spheres of human life; economics, morals, education, the Church, private relations, and public life. We must bear in mind that throughout the nineteenth and twentieth centuries, but mostly during the post-war period, the functions of the state have been gradually and almost inevitably enlarged. The state began to regulate the sphere of private relations a long time ago; several years ago, too, it began to interfere in social and economic conflicts, and to extend its control to the family, the school, the Press, public initiative and even to the Church. Life itself has been undermining the system of classical Liberalism in which the purpose of the state was purely technical. More and more the

---

[1] See Keyserling's *La Révolution Mondiale*.
[2] A term used by A. Smend in *Verfassung und Verfassungsrecht*.

D

state has ceased to be "neutral," as it was supposed to be under a secularized type of civilization. Apart, therefore, from the ideology of modern "étatisme" (which, by the way, never attains at the present time the degree of state absolutism maintained by Hegel in his doctrine of the state) we shall have to admit that "étatisme," as we see it now, is nothing new, but that it is merely a development and an exaggeration of something which already existed. If we are to set aside the totalitarian claims of the contemporary dictatorships, we shall have to admit that modern "étatisme," even in its revolutionary activity, *does not trangress* the boundaries of law. Even in the cases where "étatisme" destroys or trangresses this or that legal norm, it will create new ones in their stead, thus proving its will to be a lawful phenomenon.

Yet it is in its totalitarian tendencies, in the very theory of the "totalitarian state,"[1] that "étatisme" leaves the sphere of law. Law only claims to control the *outward behaviour* of man; it does not claim the right to control his inner life. Totalitarian tendencies, however, claim the right to influence and control man's inner life. But this life lies outside the framework of law, and is governed by the totalitarian *idea*, by the scheme which, in its historical roots, and in its very essence, can be traced to that conception of history and of man which was brought into the world by Christianity.

THE TOTALITARIAN IDEA

The totalitarian idea, as it has been proclaimed by Christianity, is a call to an *organic completeness* (totality),[2]

---

[1] See O. Spann: *Der Totale Staat.*

[2] The Russian word "tselostnost" has been introduced by the Slavophiles, more precisely by Khomiakoff. We suggest "organic completeness" as the nearest translation of it.

both in all social relations and in man himself. This idea is nothing less than the mystical and historical doctrine of the Church, as developed by Saint Paul, which strives to introduce, by means of brotherly relations, an *organic structure* into all social groups, the family, and the community. (At that time the state had not been taken into account; it was only in the Middle Ages that the idea of transforming the state into the Church arose.) This "organic structure" means a functional and vital unity, such as we see in living organisms. It is in virtue of this conception that from the early days of Christianity the family has been regarded as a "small Church," and that the Early Christian community for ever remains a type and an ideal of Church life. (This ideal is present in the type of an ideal "parish.")

More important and more complicated, however, was the change wrought by Christianity in private life as well as in the very conception of man. Christian anthropology (a doctrine which has not yet found its complete development and expression) is not a mere continuation and development of the anthropology of Scripture, with its basic ideas of the "image of God" in man and of original sin. The main emphasis in Christian anthropology lies on the doctrine of *salvation*, which opened the way for the restoration of the inner *organic completeness* which had been lost by the Fall, but belonged to man as created by God. The Fathers of the Church (and especially St. Athanasius the Great) described this process of restoration by the term "theosis." This doctrine, however, was fully aware of the actual dualism in man—the light and the darkness which wars within his nature. (This was especially emphasized in the teaching of St. Macarius the Great.) This Christian doctrine of the dualism in man— the image of God and original sin, the spirit and the flesh, life eternal and life subject to death—has nothing in com-

mon, save terminology, with that ancient dualism which
regarded the *flesh* as the source of all that is irrational,
mortal, and passionate. Christianity, on the other hand,
is based entirely on the idea of the resurrection of the flesh,
and this radically changes the very conception of "flesh."
The way to the restoration of *organic completeness* in man is
the way of mystical transfiguration through repentance,
and not through an empirical growth in perfection or an
ascetic process of self-development. No "magic of deeds"
can either effect a transfiguration of personality or van-
quish the actual dualism in man. Unity with God and
transfiguration through grace can alone achieve this. In
the light of this teaching on the way to achieve *organic
completeness* in man, Christianity gives a new interpretation of the mystery of human freedom (*mysterium libertatis*).
Freedom is, of course, connected with the mystery of
individuality as such, for personality confirms and reveals
itself only in freedom; yet, according to the Christian
doctrine, as expressed by our Lord Himself, we are fully
free only when we "know the Truth, and the Truth shall
make you free" (John viii. 32). The gift of freedom[1] cannot
of course be taken away from man even when he is inclined towards evil; this formal freedom of "choice"
means something negative and stands for freedom of
choice alone. The gift of freedom reveals itself as a creative
force only when we are united with God and abide in Him.
If we live apart from God and see no value in things
divine, our heart is divided "for where your treasure is
there will your heart be also" (Matt. vi. 21). Such division
of heart strengthens the dark element of self which stands
in opposition to the light and goodness of God, which is
still operative within us although it is constantly being
weakened by "sin that dwelleth in me" (Rom vii.17).

[1] For the further development of this subject see my essay, "The
Gift of Freedom" (in Russian), Paris 1932.

Christian *organic completeness* is not something that is given us, it is something that we have yet to attain, and the gift of freedom, while immutable in its formal content, is completely revealed only in the measure that we give ourselves up to light and goodness.

Christianity calls man to an inner *organic completeness*, to the purification and transfiguration of the heart, and not merely to "good behaviour." Christianity conceives such transfiguration of the heart as a life in God, that is, a life in the Church, the mystical body of Christ. In other words, Christianity teaches us that the creative power of freedom is revealed not in the isolation of human beings from each other, but in a brotherly union of all in Christ. Freedom, while rooted in the profound depths of personality, in its unique individuality, is not given to the isolated individual, but to the many in mystical union through brotherly love—in other words, it is given to the Church. This is the Christian "totalitarian idea" which applies to man in the completeness and unity of his outer and his inner life, and not merely to his behaviour alone. Further, the Christian totalitarian idea does not apply to the isolated individual, but to the living human community, to the organic unity of the Church.

THE FATE OF THE TOTALITARIAN IDEA

It would be out of place here to trace in detail the growth of this idea in the history of Christian nations; this story has already been told many times, and told well. I would merely remind the reader that in the Middle Ages the totalitarian idea was strongly emphasized, but in a very one-sided way, *at the expense of individual freedom*; personality was given no opportunity for free development; the Church may be said to have engulfed personality; the Church determined the whole world-view as well as the

actual modes of life, without the individual having any
part in the process. Thus the Christian message of freedom
was distorted. In this sense the whole of modern civilization was not merely a revolt against the Church, but
rather it was a return to the message of freedom. The
modern period, therefore, is saturated with the desire for
freedom and is always passionately on the defensive against
any infringement of its liberties. The key to the whole
system of secularism is separation from the Church,
liberation from her control. The whole ideology of the
"autonomy" of civilization was evolved in the name of the
freedom of personality. The experience of the Middle
Ages has borne its fruit; at the present time the Christian
consciousness will not tolerate either a return to the
medieval régime, or any infringement or deprivation
of freedom, for freedom produces and develops both a
sense of responsibility and a creative initiative of personality.

On the other hand, the Christian consciousness felt it
could not reject the totalitarian idea; therefore, even to
this very day the Christian mind feels a certain inclination towards a "New Medievalism."[1] Yet the whole of
the modern period was controlled by the spirit of secularism, that is, it rejected totalitarianism in all its forms,
both personal and social.

THE CRISIS OF SECULARISM

Strictly speaking, secularism was not anti-Christian. It
was merely anti-ecclesiastical in the sense that it rejected
the totalitarian claims of the Church and led the activity of
the Church into the channels of legal norms. One of the
new tasks of the state has been to be both an expression
and a defence of "neutrality," that is, to ensure equal

[1] See Nicolas Berdyaev: *The New Middle Ages.*

freedom to all manifestations of civilized life From the point of view of law, this established a certain balance in the mutual relations between the different spheres of civilized life and secured comparative harmony. For the Church, however, with its intrinsic purpose of embracing the whole of life—personal, social, historical—this constituted a real persecution, a painful and trying hindrance to the expression of its creative forces.

The Church has endured and is still enduring this oppression. But life, based on the principles of secularism, contained within itself the germs of a serious disease, an accumulation of poisonous and fatal elements which inclined it towards nihilism. That civilization which was conceived as the creation of free personality when it was separated from the Church, was gradually broken up into numerous separate independent spheres. It was impossible to compensate for this inner disintegration of civilization by raising personality to the level of an absolute. Religion and morality, social duties and submission to law, loyalty to the nation and a responsible participation in common life—all this has gradually lost its autonomy and become the "property" of personality[1] ,which was recognized to be free in everything. The attempt to found a super-individualism along the lines of transcendentalism, a scheme that would limit freedom of personality "from above" (Kant and Kantianism), did not go beyond the sphere of philosophy, and history continued to tend more and more toward relativism and even scepticism, and consequently toward a "dehumanization" of life, to use an expression of Nicolas Berdyaev.

Liberty proved to be most ambiguous in the midst of this development along the lines of secularism. First of all, the *historical* reality of freedom (not as it was declared

---

[1] *The Ego and His Own*, by Stirner.

by the system of law) appeared to be quite negligible.[1] Still more fatal and more dreadful was the fact that evil grew and developed at the expense of freedom, and sometimes even in its name, while the growth of the good was insignificant and languid. Freedom, separated from its religious roots, inclined towards evil, rather than towards good, towards licence rather than towards loyalty to good impulses. Good, according to an expression of V. Solovieff, became "suspect" as to its actual strength, and needed "justification"[2] as a way of creativeness and active participation in life. Such a bitter admission of the impotence of good on the basis of freedom led to the development of the revolutionary spirit, of an idealistic scheme which aimed at achieving historical and social good by means of coercion, that is, it attempted to create an order in which freedom of personality would be so limited from *without*, that evil would become impossible. The same spirit, feeling that good was not sufficiently "guaranteed" by the régime of personal freedom, pointed to another solution, which consisted in the limitation of freedom *from within* by means of *education*, that is, in the achieving of a state in which personality would no longer choose between good and evil, but would strive after good alone. Personality would thus be deprived of the gift of freedom. These are the conclusions of secularism, which revealed themselves long before the war. The war had only to lay bare all the emptiness and sterility of the whole system of civilization based on these conclusions.

MODERN DICTATORSHIPS AND THE TOTALITARIAN TENDENCIES WITHIN THEM

Neither faith in freedom, nor democracy, nor the ideology of the enlightment, proved to be able to defend goodness,

[1] See Nicolas Berdyaev: *The Fate of Man in the Modern World.*
[2] V. Solovieff's main work on ethics is *The Justification of Good.*

order, and unity; all these did not, of course, die out completely, yet they became the lot of a minority, which sought comfort in calling itself a "cultural *élite.*" The return to historical health has proved to be possible—and no sound observer of modern times could deny it—only *through power.* Herein lies the historical inevitableness, if one may say so, the historical "justification" for dictatorships, which we see to-day in great and in small nations, a tendency which penetrates (though it be in a disguised form) even into those few countries which still remain faithful to democracy.

Yet having received a "mandate" for the cleansing of life, contemporary dictatorships (in a greater or smaller measure, and almost always against their own will) have become an expression of the profound reaction against the old system of civilization. They have thus been forced to bring about the change in civilization for which the spirit of the day is longing. The totalitarian tendencies, as an ideological phenomenon, as the hidden operation of the possible future renaissance of Christianity, found themselves *forced* into contemporary dictatorships. Even now, as before, the totalitarian *idea*, in its depth, is connected with Christianity, but the totalitarian *tendencies* (whose significance it is hard to comprehend unless we bear in mind their roots in the totalitarian idea), although in most cases they present this idea in a one-sided manner, and often disfigure it, are still to be taken as evidence of the fact that Christian forces have not ceased to operate in history. This may sound like a paradox—the existence of totalitarian tendencies in modern dictatorships means that we have entered upon a new epoch in civilization.

The most significant elements in this new process, as we see it, are: the struggle with individualism, with the absolute claims of personality, as well as with the division of civilization into a series of independent spheres. Inward

and outward *organic completeness*, even though it be taken
in a limited sense, is a theme of the "new man," for whose
emergence all are longing to-day—both those in power
and the ideologists of contemporary movements. This is
why modern dictatorships instinctively, and therefore the
more insistently and passionately, *stake all on the younger
generation*. We may expect the adult to be outwardly loyal
to the new slogans; under certain circumstances we may
even expect sincere enthusiasm on their part. But the
task of achieving a new type of civilization cannot be
accomplished by such means—it requires "new men,"
and this is why those who wield authority struggle so
desperately and so passionately to capture the younger
generation.

UTOPIAN IDEAS IN PEDAGOGY

These efforts to create "new men" are not inspired in the
very least by any belief in the mystical rejuvenation of
man at which Christianity aims in its call to repentance.
The totalitarian movements of the present day do not
begin by preaching repentance, nor do they lead to
repentance. This is why they not only reject Christian
elements with scorn but they are bitterly hostile to them,
for the totalitarian movements themselves desire, in some
degree at least, to take the place of the Church.

The general educational plan (which was visionary in
the extreme from start to finish) consists in creating
(in a certain degree, in keeping with the recipes of
"Émile") a kind of educational hothouse for the young,
in which they are isolated in air-tight compartments and
thus shielded from the storms and the chaos of the present
day. The aim of this system is to prevent them from
developing a critical mind; thus they are provided with a
one-sided environment; a certain philosophy of life,

imposed from above, is instilled into them; and thus the gift of freedom is fettered from within and used only in one given direction. It would be a mistake to think that contemporary dictatorships are concerned simply with the repression of freedom in the younger generation— such an attitude does not exist. What actually happens is this: a conscious or unconscious attempt is made to shield youth from the possibility of and the necessity for choice; having eliminated the alternatives, the authorities hope that the younger people will accept the views of their elders without criticism, and that willingly and even passionately they will strive to realize the ideals which they have been taught. There is no desire to suppress or deny the gift of freedom; what the authorities desire is but to capture it, and, of course, to capture and use it *solely for their own purposes*. This is the Utopian plan which is the fatal result of the effort to dethrone personality regarded as an absolute, or in other words, to get rid of the individualism which lay at the root of the former system of culture. To a great extent authority is ready to yield to the younger generation, but only on condition that the latter is well under its control. The attention of the authorities, therefore, is mainly directed towards the various youth organizations rather than to the schools. Thus dictatorships great and small are seeking support for their Utopian system for the education and re-education of youth. The authorities, with stubborn insistence, strive to penetrate into the realm of education. Finding almost no resistance—because of the long-standing crisis in which it stands—the authorities seek to impose their own policy in an austere and sometimes even a harsh spirit.

GENERAL REMARKS ON THE AUTONOMY OF PEDAGOGY

In connection with the general development of secularism, and of the principle of the autonomy of the different spheres of culture in the nineteenth century, this principle also penetrated into pedagogy. Owing to the development of the science of psychology, and more particularly of child psychology, educational thought was inspired by the idea of the inherent powers which operate in the development of the child. In the realm of education the idea of freedom was emphasized with peculiar force, along the lines of Rousseauism. In fact, it was Rousseau who introduced the idea that the nature of the child "as such" is wholly directed towards the good, that evil reactions, moral delinquencies, and criminal tendencies arise in the child's soul only as a result of the influence of his environment, that is, of that "unnatural" mode of life which is the actual content of our so-called civilization. This faith in a "natural" direction of the child's soul toward good leaves no place for the doctrine of original sin. Hence the idea of freedom captured the realm of education and for a long time (indeed, almost down to our own day) this idea was regarded as the key to all the problems of education.

The unhappy results of secular culture, however, to which we have already referred have undermined from within man's faith in the salutary power of freedom, in his natural tendency towards good. The supreme place of personality in cultural ideology led educationalists to the idea that the most important task is to ensure the development of all the natural forces and gifts of personality, after which personality should itself freely determine its line of action. Thus, the main principle became *not the ensuring of good in children, but the ensuring of their freedom.* This gradually led to the degeneration of pedagogy into anarchy (Tolstoy and various of his followers), and assigned to pedagogy a purely "functional" task, namely, that of developing all the powers and functions of a child, and then leaving him free to choose his own way. Of its own accord the school adopted the principle of "neutrality," in order to avoid imposing any restrictions on the freedom of the child. In the name of freedom it has been considered inadmissible to lead a child in a certain definite spiritual direction. This inner self-deprivation of pedagogy was the direct result of its "autonomy." A "secret secularism" reigned in the sphere of education; the same "flowers of evil" which flourished so abundantly outside of the sphere of education began to appear within it.

When the first signs of a reaction against the old system of culture appeared, the realm of education was the first to be threatened. It is a very significant fact that A. Ferrière, the acknowledged head of the "free education movement," in his book *Le Progrès Spirituel* (1927) does not speak of the *freedom* of the child but of the *liberation* of the child, that is, of the development in him of the gift of freedom, and of the inward transfiguration of freedom by the ideals of truth and goodness. Both the Soviet and the National-Socialist education systems, although they differ from each other fundamentally, both in ideology and method, have expressed their new ideas with great force in their conception of freedom, a conception which differs in principle from that of "autonomous pedagogy."

EDUCATIONAL THEORY AND METHOD IN
SOVIET RUSSIA

I do not propose to enter here into the details or the history of Soviet pedagogical theory. It is not necessary here, and, moreover, much has already been written on this subject[1]. More essential to our purpose is a clear understanding of the object of the "cultural revolution" which was directed by a peculiar totalitarian idea and carried out in school policy. "Integral" Communism concerned itself with far more than a change in the social order. It aimed at a total transformation of all human relationships, of the fundamental world-view of every individual. The change of the social order for the Communist is but a prelude to the emancipation of man from every trace of his *bourgeois* heritage. This means that not only economic individualism must disappear, but every other kind of individualism as well. Communism, in its struggle against individualism, strives to eliminate from the very concept of personality every element tending toward self-isolation. According to Communism, personality should find its *raison d'être* only in the collective life. This, however, does not imply a total suppression of the gift of freedom, but rather a new interpretation of freedom. Communism needs daring men, with creative abilities. The element of "titanism" is one of the more obvious elements in Communism, but the idea of freedom of choice between "Communistic good" and any kind of anti-Communist (and, therefore, evil) order lies quite outside the range of possible alternatives. Free inspiration by the Communist ideal, excluding the possibility of criticism; a call for creative revolutionary "titans", of course, committed to the Communist good— these two dilemmas constitute the programme. Personality dare not lift itself above the social whole, must not oppose itself to it. Yet, on the other hand, loss of personality must be avoided.

How can the ideal of the collective be achieved without

---

[1] See also my essay: "Die Russische Pädogogik im XX Jahrhundert," in *Padagogik d. Gegenwart:* Herausgegeben von J. Schröteller, München, 1933.

sacrificing possible "titans"? How can freedom develop
without giving men opportunity for criticism? Communism tried to resolve these dilemmas by two methods:
first, by a ruthless elimination (not only in adults, but
in children also) of everything bearing the slightest trace
of the old individualism. Thus children of "non-proletarian" descent were allowed to enter neither secondary
schools nor universities. Second, all hopes were pinned
on this positive programme: the thorough grounding of
the younger generation in the *new* culture, the *new* freedom by means of "Communist education," that is, by
means of a radical refashioning, totally subject to the
state, of the entire school and extra-curricular life of the
child. The object here was more than outward mastery;
the aim was to fire the growing mind with genuine enthusiasm, to keep it at the same time under complete
control, and to make of every member of the younger
generation an obedient tool in the hands of the Party.

To this end the plan to weaken the influence of the
family was set forth with complete frankness. Traditional
Utopian schemes have always conceived of the family as
the main bulwark and teacher of "*bourgeois* individualism."
Hence, in the name of the "cultural revolution," Communism marked the family for destruction. In order to
prevent the family from exercising its "poisonous"
influence, the school, and especially the youth organizations, were called upon to serve as a wedge between parents
and children. Children were urged to oppose their parents,
to spy on them. Public "repudiation" of parents was
greatly encouraged in cases where the parents either
belonged to the old order of things or were "suspect"
by the very nature of their occupation, as in the case
of ministers of religion.

Further, Soviet educational policy, during its first
period, proclaimed a drastic campaign against educational

"humanism," against the development of the "human
being" in the child—children counted only as potential
future strugglers for the Communist order. The campaign
called for the crushing of every remnant of the humanistic
individualistic spirit. To this end the Soviet school, up
to the time of the very recent reforms, made a sharp
distinction between children of proletarian descent and
children of non-proletarian descent. By special committees
within the schools the children were enlisted to help to
further this discrimination. Only children who belonged
to Communist organizations such as the "Pioneers" or
the Young Communist League could stand near the
head of the class. The aim of the Soviet school was not to
build up "man as such," not to develop the personality
of the child, but to train and develop an active worker
for Communism, wholly devoted to the interests of the
Soviet order. Thus Communist totalitarianism invaded
the sphere of education.

This plan to capture completely the soul of youth, to
give to it a ready-made world view, a prepared set of
feelings, a definite philosophy of life, to excise all that
could not be reconciled with the Communist ideal—all
this "ideocratic" scheme with regard to the younger
generation had for its aim something which the Church
alone can achieve, the Christian Church with her message
of the restoration of man to his primitive integrity, and
her message of victory over sin. It may be noted that
"original sin" in man means *bourgeois* ideology to the
Communist. Communism repudiates also Rousseau's
theory of the "natural good" crushed by civilization.
Soviet theory believes only in "revolutionary enthusiasm"
and in this sense it emphasizes in the name of Communism
an inner "transfiguration" of man.[1] This transfiguration

[1] See the interesting book by Dévaud: *La Pédagogie Scolaire en
Russie Soviètique*, Paris, 1932.

of man had hitherto been the prerogative of the Church.

It is hardly worth while here to dwell on the system of the Soviet school. In passing we may note, for example, its conception of labour as education, its theory of the "dying off of the school," the project of the "polytechnical school," the connection of the school system with the factory, the centralization of the entire range of school work in the hands of the state. What is more important for us to bear in mind is that after the first fourteen years there came about a very strong reaction in Soviet educational policy.

THE VICTORY OF EDUCATIONAL REALISM IN SOVIET POLICY

This reaction, which bears the name of educational realism, has not yet reached its peak. By realism is meant the elimination of all Utopian elements, as well as the circumvention, partial at least, of the totalitarian tendencies which had originally determined the means and methods of Soviet education. To a large extent this is connected with the general failure of the Soviet régime, now maintained only by terror. This failure led the régime to abandon in various realms of life the principle of forcing unsuitable forms upon life processes. In the educational sphere, the "totalitarian objective" has proved to the school to be an obstacle to the fulfilment of its proper task. More and more the schools are allowed to conduct their work in accordance with "old" methods, that is, they prepare for life educated and disciplined workers. All the elements which were forcibly introduced into the school system by the totalitarian tendencies, by integral Communism, have now been shifted from the school into the youth organizations—the *Comsomol*. The

E

latter has been set free (Congress of 1936) from its former purely political objectives. Now the *Comsomol* aims at the final elimination of all traces in youth of the old *bourgeois* civilization and at the patient and gradual cultivation of "creative enthusiasm" in the younger generation. All this points to the significant fact that a simplified system of "manufacturing" a synthetic psychology for youth is now being rejected in favour of a realistic approach. The Utopian aim of forming "new men" now passes from the school to the youth organizations, leaving the school to seek its proper educational objectives (see below for the parallel process in Italy). This reflects the new realistic policy of Soviet education. To achieve their ends they no longer regard it as necessary to "drug" children, but concentrate all efforts instead toward the capture of the freedom of the child's intellect as developed by the schools. The real problem of totalitarian education thus reveals itself with greater clarity than before 1933, when Utopian schemes prevailed.

THE CONCEPTION OF COMMUNITY AND CULTURE (OR "VOLK"?) IN GERMANY

The German attempt to master the "theme of life" and to lay the foundation of a new culture and civilization in Germany, presents quite a different picture. The whole movement which has been developed under the influence of National Socialism is also determined by a reaction against the old form of culture and civilization.[1] Yet the motive is different from that which obtained in Soviet Russia. A group holding a very definite ideology is not only at the head of the state, but it is also controlling and

[1] Gottfried Benn's *Der Neue Staat und die Intellectuellen*, 1933, gives a most interesting description of the new conception of culture in present-day Germany.

guiding the thought of contemporary Germany. Owing to the complexity of the basic ideas of National Socialism, it is difficult to determine in what the main and the most effective force of this movement consists. I personally believe that emphasis should be laid not on the question of race, and not even on the mythology of "blood and soil"; to me all this does not seem to express the actual essence of the contemporary movement in Germany, and it can easily fall away without doing any harm to the fundamental principle. This basic principle is the *Völkische Idee*, which is not so much nationalism, in the usual meaning of the word, but rather *das Volkstum*, the people. Not the *nation* but the *people*; not an historical union, but the organic unity of the spirit of the people, in the same sense perhaps as the "organic" idea was understood in the days of romanticism.[1] The significant factor here is the *primacy of the people* over individual *personality*. A very important and really creative change in cultural ideology is taking place in Germany in this connection. The ideas of Krieck, an educationalist and philosopher who joined the National-Socialist movement from the very start, are most interesting in this connection. "In our day," he writes,[2] "the conception of personality has received a new significance and a new content. Personality does not mean the individual man who has achieved the development of his capacity in the desert of empty freedom. He becomes a personality who achieves his maturity through service to the whole, that is, to the people. This maturity confers upon him the gift of vision, opens up before him a wide field of action with responsible tasks. A personality necessarily becomes a leader, and *outside of this* we neither know nor recognise personality." It would be a mistake to believe that this is

---

[1] Adam Müller and others.

[2] E. Krieck, *Nationalsozialistische Erziehung*, 1933, p. 10.

only a chance phrase of Krieck's, a *lapsus linguae*. Such a doctrine of personality is in line with the *Ganzheits-gedanke*,[1] that is, it is in line with totalitarian tendencies, which dominate the contemporary mind. While the individualist of the past epoch proceeded from the separate "I" and thus turned the people into a mere sum total of personalities, leaving no room for the idea of the organic structure of the whole—here we see the effect of the other extreme—the primacy of the whole leads to the admission that not every individual is a personality (or may become such as his character develops), but only one to whom it is given to be a "leader" in the emphasis of some truth, large or small. This statement contains both a great truth and a great falsehood, for a paradoxical blending of truth and falsehood is generally characteristic of the totalitarian tendencies of our day.

It is true that ontologically personality does not precede the whole. By asserting this, we set ourselves free from the mistake of classical individualism, which naturally led to the enthronement of personality, to atomization, to all the blind alleys of "isolation." Personality "finds itself" in the whole, and this whole is, of course, the people—yet personality forms itself in every individual, and not in "leaders" alone. For if it is the sense of responsibility which forms personality, this is a responsibility not to the people, and not even to the state, but to that which dominates both people and state, that which is not subject to relative standards set up by history. Transcendental philosophy called it by the term "sphere of values," whereas we Christians assert that personality is formed only in fellowship with God in its religious "action."

How can *das Volkstum*, which is built up and destroyed in history, which lives through periods of crisis and decay and often moves in wrong directions, be made into an

[1] E. Krieck, *Nationalsozialistische Erziehung*, 1933, p. 18.

absolute? *Das Volkstum* is relative, even more than anything else—*it is historic* in its very essence. And, therefore,
responsibility to *das Volkstum* can by no means be, as
Krieck would maintain, that element which *forms* personality. The truth here is this: personality is formed
through communion with the super-personal principle;
to look for this principle in the people, is to make the
formation of personality dependent upon a basis which
is variable and often sinful and diseased. Further, can the
whole of personality be exhausted by its own activity in
the name and for the sake of the people? Even if this
people were unique in the world, or if it were to become
the whole of humanity, even then the human spirit cannot finally spend itself in history; it demands and seeks
for the eternal, the super-historical. It can be truly said,
that only he serves his people who lifts his service above
the conventions and relativisms of historical life, who
lights the spirit of his people by his own reverence for
eternal truth, eternal good—for God.

In its search for a new civilization, in its endeavour to
overcome the faults of the preceding epoch, the new
ideology in Germany has utilized totalitarian tendencies,
and strives to evoke in man all that enthusiasm which
comes from identification with a whole—the people. By
this means the new German ideology seeks to solve the
problem of freedom, to remove its sting, to eliminate its
element of possible rebellion, the poison of self-determined
isolation, and at the same time to fire the soul of man with
genuine enthusiasm. Here—as in all other "ideocracies"
—all hopes are laid not on adults, but on youth. It follows
that education becomes the focal point for the realization
of these hopes. Education is expected to excise all rem-
nants of the past, to bring forth the "new man," to create
an "integral man" who gives himself up completely in
creative service to his people, a man who knows no selfish-

ness, who has no inner struggles and misgivings, who always follows the "line" set forth by the "leader."

Since the schools submitted supinely to authority, the attempt to capture the younger generation for the new civilization shifted its attention to the problem of extramural youth organizations. These youth organizations, strong because of Germany's traditional *Jugendbewegung*, the state has determined to dominate completely, making them channels of the "cultural revolution"; the driving force of National Socialism. To achieve this, there was decreed a centralization of all youth organizations in the hands of the state. As in Italy, all sports organizations, all the physical training of the young people, are centred in the state. This is a very characteristic feature of totalitarian procedure—sport has for some time held a large place in contemporary civilization. The processes of "integration" operate with especial force in all that is connected with sport—in private, national, and even international life. While this is a prominent symbol of contemporary life, it does not imply barbarization or any regress in civilization. On the contrary it is involved in the reaction against the past epoch, against its intellectualism, its loss of organic unity with nature, its disavowal of the "integral nature" in man.[1]

In its endeavour to win youth, to bring about its voluntary acceptance of the new ideology, to conquer "the heart of youth," National Socialism strives to convince every young person that personality receives its force and its freedom *only through identification with the Volksgeist*.[2] Those in authority say, in other words, that personality mystically depends upon *Volksgeist*. This "organic" doctrine ascribes to the people exactly that which Christianity believes to be the attribute of the

[1] On this see the interesting book by G. Giese: *Geist im Sport*.
[2] Compare with Winfrid: *Sinnwandel d. formalen Bildung*, 1935.

Church. In place, however, of spiritual unity, which is the Church, this *Volksmythologie* gives us unity of "blood and soil."

We stated above our conviction that the creative energies of National Socialism are found not in its theory of race, but rather in its search for a super-individual reality, in union with which personality overcomes its isolation. By this union also the inner chaos of freedom is overcome, and freedom without chaos, by its release of creative energies, fills personality with a power transcending individual power. In order to dominate personality, to inspire personality, the people must assume that significance hitherto held by "humanity in general."[1] From this line of thought is derived the idea of the supreme "sovereignty," the "totality" of people and state.[2] The individual man enters into a deep (mystical) union with his people, with the state, through his devotion to the state (*Staatsgesinnung*). He thus achieves a "rejuvenation" of personality, he is liberated from the evil effects of the epoch of individualism.

EDUCATION AND STATE IN ITALY

I should like to add a few words concerning Italy. In Italy educational reforms are more free from artificial pressure upon youth. Even here, however, the state—which is recognized as the supreme super-individual value—strives to become the exclusive object of love and service. Here, too, education is commissioned to take possession of the child's freedom by filling his soul with enthusiasm, with heroic impulse. The Italian system does not interfere with family life, does not hinder the Church in the latter's task of religious education of the children,

---

[1] Giese, *Staat und Erziehung*, speaks (p. 33) of the "Tyranny of the humanity idea."   [2] Ibid., p. 151.

but directs its attention to organized sport. As early as 1923 the physical education of children and youth was separated from the school in order to centre supervision in the hands of the state. In 1926 the "Opera Ballila" was founded, and a year later this organization was entrusted with leadership of the whole system of physical training of children. This effectively removed control over such training from the Ministry of Education. Now all children and adolescents in Italy between the ages of 6 and 18 form an organization which, while having physical training as its basis, aims at capturing the soul of youth. As a means of attaining this objective, the school, in its educational capacity, is almost ignored. The chief "problem of the new culture," that is, the overcoming of individualism and the "directing and governing" of the freedom of youth (without, however, suppressing that freedom), falls for solution to the organizations for children and youth. By concentrating entire control in the hands of the state, the exclusive influence of the state in all phases of this work is ensured. Besides, the physical education basis of all these organizations marks them as belonging to the "new epoch."

THE PRIMARY EMPHASIS IN TOTALITARIAN POLICY

As has already been pointed out, the totalitarian tendencies in contemporary life constitute the reaction against the entire preceding cultural epoch, rather than any crisis in education considered by itself. In spite of this wider basis, the totalitarian tendencies exert their chief force in the sphere of education.

We must bear in mind, first of all, that centralization, as such, in the hands of the state, of all education both inside and especially outside the school, is not the *goal* of totalitarian policy. It is rather a means toward the achievement of a goal of more profound character. Suppression of private initiative, forcing the family into the background, handicapping or eliminating the Church in its work with children and youth—all this is not an independent reality, but the *manifestation* and the *expression* of forces of deeper significance.

The aim is, fundamentally, to bring about a new type, a new pattern of culture, through complete control of the school and all youth organizations: a new civilization with new ideology, eliminating individualistic isolation and the old concept of freedom, demanding not only exclusive loyalty to the "whole" but enthusiastic love as well. The meaning of the "whole"—party, state, people— varies, of course, in different nations. The central purpose in these new experiments in education is a controlled development of all the capacities of man, which without suppressing the gift of freedom would direct this freedom toward ways pointed out from above.

RELATIVE SUCCESS OF THE TOTALITARIAN PLAN IN EDUCATION

Any evaluation of this totalitarian plan so far must admit its *relative success* as education. At this date, of course, any *general* conclusion as to the results of the totalitarian experiment in education would be premature and even unwarranted. On the other hand, one cannot deny that the different states have achieved many of their objectives. In Italy the system of Fascism has always been free from the excesses which characterize the German and Soviet régimes. All unprejudiced observers agree that Italian youth is enthusiastically devoted to the Duce and fully accepts the official ideology. It is another matter as to whether this state of affairs is either stable or permanent —any answer on this point must be only tentative. In

Germany, too, the younger generation enthusiastically follows those in power.

We must admit, with certain definite reservations, that Soviet Russia, too, has met with some success at this point. When dealing with Soviet Russia, however, it is more difficult to establish a correct "hierarchy of facts," yet one cannot deny either that vast numbers of young people wholeheartedly share *a great part* of the "credo" of the party, or that, disregarding the presence of a great deal of "ordered" enthusiasm and conviction dictated from above, there does exist a real "creative *extase*," as well as a genuine enthusiasm with regard to the titanic plans and slogans coming from official circles.

What is the price, however, of this relative success? What is its basis? Is the problem of the new epoch actually solved in the realm of education?

UTILIZATION OF YOUTH'S LOVE OF SPORT

Youth's love of sport provides the positive basis of the "relative success" achieved in the sphere of education by the totalitarian tendencies. The emergence of this preoccupation with sport is no superficial phenomenon. It has deep roots in a *spiritual* change in life.[1] As contrasted with the abstract intellectualism, and the false attitude toward physical life held during the past epoch, love of sport is in itself an expression of a desire for a natural "organic completeness" of life.

By the assistance and control of youth organizations, the dictatorships easily capture the younger generation. The same is true in democratic countries where this movement has gained a foothold. In this process, however, it is not so much youth who are conquered by the authorities, but rather the latter who follow the lead of youth. All this

---

[1] See G. Giese's *Geist im Sport*, referred to above.

should be borne in mind in order to make a correct evaluation of the resulting phenomenon and not to over-estimate the "achievements" of those in power.

The fact that youth occupies the centre of attention provides another very significant factor in the capture of youth by authority. While the preceding epoch paid but little attention to the younger generation, youth sees to-day all doors open before it. In addition, totalitarian tendencies are congenial to the temper of contemporary youth. This implies a momentous change in modern social history, a development quite independent of any particular régime, and even of any particular authoritative plans. Even the over-developed nationalism which animates most states, and especially the dictatorial states, finds a very real response on the part of the young. It is true that a number of *negative* elements provide the basis of this widespread response of youth to authority. This is especially obvious in Germany, where hatred of the Versailles Treaty proved to be a powerful factor in bring-ing about unity between the authorities and the people, young and old. In Soviet Russia the idea of "foreign intervention" is carefully cultivated in the minds of every-one, for the purpose of reviving and strengthening this same national sentiment. The "Abyssinian episode," which, to a very great extent, isolated Italy from the rest of the world, greatly helped to bring about an inner unity of the authorities with the people.

THE UNREALITY OF THE TOTALITARIAN SOLUTION OF THE PROBLEM

Without making any prophecy, we have grounds to affirm that the "relative success" of the totalitarian experiments in the realm of education conceals an unreal solution to the problem of the epoch. The entire question rests fundamentally on the problem of freedom. It is quite possible to circumscribe freedom or to give it direction, but under no circumstances does this lead to the creation of a new cultural epoch, nor does it provide a solution to the basic problem with which our age so painfully struggles. Of course, man is free to circumscribe his freedom, but this way leads only to slavery and to degeneration, and signifies a renunciation of the achievements of civilization. If, however, we desire to preserve freedom in the heart of man and, at the same time, to provide safeguards against the atomization which is unavoidable under the old individualism—then we must openly proclaim that the solution of this problem is possible only on the religious plane— in and through the Church.

TOWARDS A NEW EPOCH

There is, of course, another way out, namely that of trying to amend and correct the content and method of the preceding epoch by a series of compromises. It is possible that history may choose this particular way, yet it is evident that a solution through compromise does not eliminate the main defect, the fundamental error of the preceding epoch. If it is both senseless and inadmissible to suppress freedom, it is also wrong to believe that it is possible to overcome the inner chaos in freedom by means of partial limitations and external safeguards. This chaos can finally be overcome only along the line of a *free desire for such limitation*, that is, through self-limitation, self-discipline. All the totalitarian experiments of the day admit this, to a certain extent, in so far as they strive to evoke the "enthusiasm of the masses" to undergird their programmes. Yet this artificially stimulated enthusiasm *cannot last for ever*—it unavoidably calls forth an opposite reaction. In such "enthusiasm" it is fruitless to seek the key to the one true protection of the gift of freedom from chaos and inclination to evil. This achievement results only from self-discipline, it follows the inner struggle *which can never be decreed* from above.

In the end, the state authority cannot solve the problem of the new epoch: totalitarian schemes derive their historical meaning and act creatively only because of their implicit religious basis. One can, of course, doubt whether we, in our time, have now actually entered the period of "the Christian Renaissance," yet whether we have or not, we are bound to maintain that, if the basic crisis of this epoch can in any wise be overcome, *this will come about not through the state's interference in cultural processes, but through the Church's assumption of her full responsibility for the character of civilization.* The development of this theme lies outside the scope of the present study.

THE PROBLEM OF EDUCATION AND THE "NEW EPOCH"

No one would counsel abandoning all that is true and valuable in the past system of education. The personality of the child should be developed to the utmost of his capacities. Creative initiative, strength of character, consciousness of responsibility, must continue to receive attention. But granting this, the first concern is that the gift of freedom be developed through its inner illumination by the spirit. The key to the new education lies here: the Church must take up her educational responsibility for the spiritual illumination of personality. This means neither the suppression of freedom nor the limitation of freedom by reason, or by grafting on good habits, or by evoking an outburst of artificial enthusiasm—freedom finds its limitation only in the development of the spiritual life in the name of Christ the Saviour.

By introducing the meaning of Christianity into the soul of the child, by imparting to the child the power of grace dwelling in the Church, by awakening in his soul a Christian consciousness, and finally by developing his inner spiritual life through awareness of the fact that he is in the presence of God, and by humble submission to the Will of God—in this way and in this way alone shall we illumine the gift of freedom—through its development and not through its limitation.

RELATIONSHIP OF COMMUNITY, STATE, GOVERNMENT, CHURCH, AND SCHOOL IN THE UNITED STATES

by

PAUL MONROE
Columbia University, New York

RELATIONSHIP OF COMMUNITY, STATE, GOVERNMENT, CHURCH, AND SCHOOL IN THE UNITED STATES

THE systems of education characteristic of the present generation may be roughly classified as three. These correspond with the systems of political and social organizations which dominate the present. But these educational systems also embody, as do the political, social, and economic systems, those forces or tendencies which are characteristic of the past.

The first of these systems is that prevailing in most continental European countries. In these countries education is a function of government. The educational system was created and is now controlled by government for the purpose of maintaining the government structure and function. That function is primarily the maintenance of the national culture and the development of a national ideal.

Education is thus the chief force upon which government depends for the realization of national group ideals. The extreme and most characteristic expressions of this form of education are those found in the totalitarian states of Germany, Italy, and Russia. Due to the process by which the educational system was evolved this attitude of complete control of education by government is true of most other continental European countries. It is also found for the most part in those countries where the social system is an offspring of continental Europe, as in the countries of Latin America, and in those countries where the educational system was developed largely on the model of the educational system of these continental European countries. This includes the educational systems of most Oriental countries. One essential factor if not

F

the most essential factor in these European countries is that in the past education was wholly in the hands of the Church, as the Church was the dominant institution for the realization of the cultural ideals of the nation. As the conception of an education universally effective developed, this function of education was gradually handed over to the government by the Church.

The second type of educational system, that most in contrast with the one described above, is that found in Great Britain. Even in Great Britain one must revert to the eighteenth century or the early part of the nineteenth century to find this type in its clearest form. Here education is fundamentally an individual activity for the purpose of achieving individual standards of culture, usually expressed in terms of free personality. While this conception prevails in its clearest form, government has little to do with educational activities. Such activities are left to individual effort or to the effort of self-constituted and self-dependent groups. The Church, though powerful in its influence, no longer controls directly; the government interferes but slightly, and that only recently to make more universal the incidence of education.

The third type, if not a compromise between the other two extremes, at least lies midway between them. Government interferes to prevent the Church or any other external force from controlling education; lays some kind of restriction upon itself and gives control, support, and determination of the character of education to the state or to local groups. In other words, Government itself endeavours to keep its hands off education and leave to expressions of the state other than political government the formulation and control of educational procedures. This midway type is characteristic of the United States. As with the second type this is found in its clearest form before the present generation; the experiences of the last generation have introduced new tendencies into all three types. In order to see clearly the characteristics one must revert to the period of development.

Other papers in this series have been prepared to present the characteristic features of the first and second types mentioned above. It is the purpose of this paper to explain the characteristics of the third type as they can be explained through historical development. It is no purpose of this paper to present a philosophical analysis or philosophical defence of this system. While the writer believes whole-heartedly in the validity of the system, this attitude is probably because he is the product of that system and has passed his professional life in the operation and promotion of that system.

Before proceeding with the attempt at historical analysis it is desirable to define some essential terms, particularly as, at times, they are given a different meaning in these papers. The terms government, state, nation, community, administration are essential to a clear understanding of these types, but in their use these terms are often confused. It must be admitted that they do not possess a clear distinction in common use; yet their meaning as used must be made clear, because this exposition of the character of the three types of education depends to a large extent upon the consistent use of these terms. In the English use of the term "government" usually means the existing political administration. But this meaning in the United States is usually expressed by the word "administration." In American usage the term "government" usually means the political organization of the state, and includes both federal and local government. This American distinction makes for a common misunderstanding of American life by those of other cultural backgrounds. The commonest form of political expression

of the American "state" is through constitutional conventions. Such conventions are political expressions of
the "state" but are not part of the "government."
Yet the ideals which such constitutional conventions
create become a part of the "government" as do the
legislative and executive branches of the government
which conventions also create.

The American use of these terms is yet further complicated by the use of the term "state" in common parlance
to indicate any one of the forty-eight commonwealths
which constitute the federal union. This usage but indicates that originally the commonwealths or colonies were
independent and that when sovereignty was removed
from England to America it resided in the thirteen original
colonies. The reservation of this sovereignty to the federal
union by the constitution of 1789 further perpetuated
this distinction between "state" and "government."
This paper uses the term "state" only in this sense, and
not in that of its more frequent use as synonymous with
commonwealth.

The state, then, is a political organization of the community which expresses itself politically through government, through constitutional conventions, and also,
curiously enough, through its educational system. The
American educational system becomes then an expression of the state but not of the government. State universities, educational expressions of thirty-three of the forty-
eight commonwealths, are controlled by Boards of
Regents; these Boards may be elected by the people, or
appointed by the governor, or selected by the legislature
to represent the people—that is, the state. After appointment such regents are no longer under the control of
the political appointing power and are removable only
by termination of the period of appointment, or by court
procedure. Local schools in cities or in other smaller

governmental units are controlled by school boards. Such boards are usually elected by the people directly, always so in the case of local government units other than municipalities. In municipalities often the mayor appoints representatives of the people, that is, of the state. Such appointees again may only be removed by expiration of term or by order of court for incompetence or unfitness for office.

In Professor Clarke's paper the term "community" is constantly used to mean a group of people voluntarily associating themselves for some cultural purpose, or it may mean local government. In the United States when a community organizes for the support or control of schools it is the state through which it operates.

The community as a voluntary organization, as a religious or denominational group also exists in the United States, and frequently, especially in the past, organized and supported schools. The large increase in parochial schools in recent years would indicate that this type of community organization for educational purposes was not confined to the past.

The problem of terms is here somewhat further complicated by the fact that some powers are delegated. For example, the power of licensing teachers may be and usually is assigned to some agency set up by the government. So also is the function of supervision. The legislature as a branch of government also frequently prescribes the content of education. These functions then become illustrative of the way in which education is gradually passing step by step under the control of government. All this may yet be changed by the assertion of the fundamental power of the state as opposed to the delegated or enumerated power of government.

This conflict is essentially the basis of the present-day political controversy in the United States, a controversy that is so confusing to those outside of the American system and indeed confusing to Americans also.

On the basis of this distinction between the people or "community," the "state" and "government" two points of significance emerge. First, how did these distinctions, especially in their bearing on education, develop? Second, what is the resulting relationship between "state," "government," "church," and "education"? So far as European countries are concerned, the problem is usually between "government," "church," and "education." But so far as the United States is concerned, the main point of the situation is missed unless the term "state" is also included.

Even at the expense of a rather tedious discussion, let us address ourselves to the answer to the first question: how did this distinction between "state," "government," and the individual or community and education develop in the United States, so that a situation quite different from that in England or on the Continent is to be found?

No doubt it is chiefly due to the fact that for two and a half centuries the American colonies were accustomed to recognizing the sovereignty of the state existing in Europe; that the government was immediately at hand; and that the community or the people and their interests were distinct from both and for the most part hostile to both. When the colonies or communities asserted their rights by revolution they assumed sovereignty and removed it from Europe to America. In the formulation of the American state the common sentiment revealed itself quite as hostile to government as it did to the remote European sovereignty.

One of the earliest clear statements of these three major social factors to be found in Colonial documents is one from Virginia in the latter part of the seventeenth century. The situation described was typical of all of those

settlements which were dominated by English sentiment and tradition. This document is that oft-quoted
reply of Governor Berkeley of Virginia in 1671 to the
inquiry from the Home Office. Such inquiries were made
from time to time in the form of a questionnaire, a procedure more familiar in the present time in educational
activities than in governmental.

While this reply is very frequently quoted it is seldom
quoted in full. The portion of the reply that bears on our
present problem is usually omitted altogether, while the
portion usually quoted leaves quite a wrong impression
concerning conditions if these conditions are not examined
outside of the document itself. The question asked in the
Home Office inquiry was: "What course is taken about
instructing the people within your government in the
Christian religion?" The reply of Governor Berkeley
was: "The same course that is taken in England, out of
town: every man according to his ability instructing his
children. But I thank God there are no free schools nor
printing, and I hope we shall not have them in a hundred years: for learning has brought disobedience and
heresy and sects in the world, and printing has divulged
them and libels against the best of governments. God keep
us from both."

The first sentence of this reply, of especial significance
for our discussion, is seldom noted, while the later sen-
tences without interpretation have often been quoted to
demonstrate the complete lack of appreciation of learning in the southern colonies. As a matter of fact, at about
the time this document was written the testy governor
was a contributor to the founding of a free school. So,
indeed, were most of the other prominent citizens. So also
did the legislature of the colony make similar pledge of
support in contributions of tobacco. Whether this free
school was ever actually in operation we have no means

of determining. But shortly afterwards others were. There had been some such schools in earlier years that had ceased to exist. It should be borne in mind also in explanation of the hostile attitude of the governor that this was at the period of the Stuart restoration which the government represented. And there was in progress in Virginia, it must be remembered, the so-called "Bacon's rebellion," against the "best of governments," as the governor saw it, as well as against the Established Church. Hence the side remark hostile to free schools and to the printing press. These remarks were really aimed at conditions in England rather than at those in America, and were literally meant for "home consumption."

The governor's first sentence is the significant portion of this exposition, "each according to his ability educating his children."

A series of laws extending throughout the colonial period supplemented the English individual system. Due to the system of indentured white servants there existed throughout the colonial period a large class of children either orphaned or without responsible parents. For all such legal enactments required parents, guardians, or vestrymen of the parish to provide schooling or training. The vestrymen of the parish were civil as well as ecclesiastical officials. However, it was the parish as a civil unit with the power to tax that assumed the responsibility.

In the New England colonies Massachusetts usually takes precedence, and is typical of the other colonies. Here in 1642 was passed probably the first general school law of the colonies. As in the south, this law laid upon the individual family the responsibility of educating its own children both in learning, that is, in reading and writing, and in craftsmanship, that is, in employment. In case the parent neglected his duty the town must assume responsibility. In doing so all the families of the town were parcelled out among the select men, the civil officers of the town. The first general school law in America was passed by Massachusetts some five years later, in 1647. The records of all the towns established before this date reveal that the law of 1642 was being faithfully executed, and also that all of these towns in order to make operative the law of 1642 had actually established schools before the law of 1647 was passed.

In the central colonies the policy of Pennsylvania was typical. Here the colony passed to the various religious bodies, chiefly Quaker and various German sects, the responsibility of educating the children both in learning and in occupation. While the procedure might be carried out as in New York by requirement that all school teachers be licensed by the governor, the general result was the same.

Hence in all three groups of colonies we find the essential American principles early formulated and differentiated from those accepted in England.

The first of these principles, the principle accepted in England, was that the primary responsibility for the education of the child rested on the parents or on the individual family. The second general principle was that the state assumed the ultimate responsibility for the general education of youth. This responsibility was assumed in the southern colonies by the vestrymen, who were representative both of the civil and of the ecclesiastical power; that is, the distinctions between state, government, church, and community were not clearly drawn, largely because the church was an established church identical with the governments; while the power of the community or of the state was not clearly differentiated from that of the sovereign power of the king as represented by the royal governor.

In the New England colonies the actual authority was

exercised by the town meeting which elected the select-men who is turn carried out the provision of the colonial law. While membership in the town meeting was for a period limited to those who were members of the church, it was also provided by law that this limitation did not apply in school affairs, which were therefore affairs to be decided by the community as organized for this purpose.

In the middle colonies the control of the schools was left to various religious sects as these corresponded to the various sections of the community.

In all sections these principles thus emerged very early, though not always clearly. The major principle was later to emerge and dominate, namely, that the state as representing all of the people was to control the educa-tion of the youth of the community, and that this control was not to be exercised by the government.

However, during this early period this relationship was not clearly defined. The government was not clearly differentiated from the state as the latter was represented in the royal charter or in an appointed governor. Nor was the colonial legislature yet distinguished as a branch of government either on one hand from the royal power, or on the other hand from the sovereign power of the people. The Great and General Court of Massachusetts was at first composed of all freemen of the colony, and in time declared itself the sovereign power. Meanwhile, as it became impossible for the scattered freemen to meet, representative delegates were accepted and representative government thus came into existence.

The following stage in the relationship of state, govern-ment, church, and education was most clearly and most early developed in Massachusetts. The development here can be taken as typical of the whole country, followed though perhaps slowly. The essential process was the assignment of the control of education to the people directly. This was done through the establishment of local schools as independent units each under the control of the people who patronized the school. Thus control was exercised through the instrumentality of the school board, in time elected directly by the people. This was achieved through stages of evolution: first the control of the select-men; then of a school committee; then of a school committee in which each member represented a school district; then of a permissive district school system; then of a compulsory district school system, each school constituting a district with the power of constituting a district board, of taxation for the support of the school, of appointment of teacher, and so on.

This system was made permissive just before the American revolution in 1768, and was made obligatory immediately following the adoption of the constitution in 1789. Though so great an authority as Horace Mann pronounced this act as the nadir of American education, the system did establish the direct control of the people over the schools, and clearly defined the state as the ultimate authority, and separated the government and the state in the thinking of the people respecting education. By making the school wholly and completely responsible to the will of the people, this system established education as the fundamental basis of democracy. By this procedure both government and church were eliminated from the control of schools.

In time, during the nineteenth century, government assumed or was delegated certain powers respecting schools. These powers included the licensing of teachers, the approval of text-books, the inspection of schools, the distribution of school funds which came from general funds or from commonwealth taxation. Such control was gained by means of the distribution of common school funds which were established in practically all common-wealths. These common school funds were in most cases established by constitutional provision, hence became acts of the state and not of the government. But the constitution also usually placed on the school authority the duty of distributing the proceeds of common school funds which lead to the power of inspection, usually in the hands of government school officials.

In the middle states a system of rate bills grew up under these conditions. The inevitable question arose many times and in many places concerning the actual authority of these respective institutions as well as the question to what extent the state or the government should include the religious element in education. The question in its most direct legal form arose in connection with the distribution of the common school funds: should such funds be allotted to sectarian or church schools? This question was fought out a number of times and in several places; particularly in the commonwealth of New York, once in the early part of the nineteenth century, and once about the middle of the century. This question was closely tied up with that of the establishment of free common schools involving the abolition of the rate bill and the substitution of school support by direct taxation. The question was settled definitely about the middle of the century by the adoption of a constitutional provision which forbade the granting of any common-wealth funds for the support of any sectarian schools. This provision laid a definite restriction on both govern-ment and church.

Elsewhere the question arose chiefly over the use of religious matters in the curriculum. Many legal decisions have been made in different communities of the country. Most of these decisions approve the prohibition of all religious instruction in the public schools. The most recent of such decisions made in the early part of the twentieth century in the commonwealth of California forbade the reading of the King James version of the Bible as a sectarian exercise. As the reasoning in this decision would apply to any translation of the Bible, all religious instruction is thus declared illegal. This decision undoubtedly is in harmony with both court decisions and with community sentiment in most regions of the country. On the other hand, one commonwealth, Mississippi, still definitely forbids by constitution any legal limitation on the use of the Bible in the school.

If any parent will bring legal action against such instruction, where it exists, the general evidence is that the courts will universally rule against the inclusion of any such instruction in the school programme. In recent years, particularly during the twentieth century, there have been many cases in which the various religious denominations of the community have united on some common programme of religious instruction usually with provision for sectarian instruction by the sect represented. Sometimes such a scheme is provided for by local commonwealth law; sometimes permitted where there is no local opposition; sometimes also existing on the basis of long-standing custom. But the major principle of complete separation of church and state and education has not been modified.

The relation of the state, government, and schools is still further complicated in the United States by the fact that all municipal governments are chartered by and hence are controlled by legislature. However, the same principle applies to the control of local school boards. In local or city school boards the members are in some cases appointed by the mayor, in some cases by the city council, in some few cases elected by the people directly; but in every case once elected or appointed they are independent of the appointing power and in all cases represent the people directly; that is, represent the state and not the government. In Great Britain a school committee is a branch of the local municipal government. Not so in the United States. The local school board is an independent organ of the state, as is the local government itself.

In the case of secondary education, such schools now exist practically universally as a part of common education. This principle was first settled by a Supreme Court ruling in the commonwealth of Michigan in 1877. In this decision secondary education was declared a part of the common school system. Early decisions in neighbouring commonwealths had declared such schools to be class schools, and hence forbidden under the constitution. At present with the practical inclusion of most children of appropriate age in secondary public schools the question no longer arises.

Most institutions of collegiate grade are under sectarian control or under the control of self-perpetuating boards that are assumed to represent the trust imposed upon them—to operate the institution in the interests of the state or of the local community which they represent. Universities are of this latter type, or are state institutions. The state universities exist in almost all of the commonwealths of the union: the term "state" in this connection means "commonwealth" not state in distinction to government. Such institutions are controlled by boards of regents, the members of which may be appointed by the governor, may be selected by legislature, or may be elected by the people directly.

In any circumstance the regents are not responsible to the appointing powers, but are responsible to the courts for the performance of the trust in the interests of the community at large. In this respect their situation is identical with that of the members of the local school board. Here again the complete separation of the state, government, and church is evident, and has been guaranteed by legal decision. The distinction between the power of the government and of the state was made in the famous Dartmouth College case in 1817. This was perhaps the most important single legal decision in the history of the country. Thus these principles have been worked out through historical evolution, though they were inherent in the early colonial situation before they became explicit. It is probable that the early colonial situation was responsible for the formulation of these principles as is discussed earlier.

The two and a half centuries of historical evolution produced little change in these fundamental principles except a sharpening of the distinctions and a closer adaptation to local conditions.

However, the present century with the profound changes brought about by the world war and the subsequent economic revolution has brought the proposal and at least the temporary acceptance of modification. Such modification if made permanent will involve a marked change in fundamental principles.

The federal government has interfered in many ways with the process of education, thus taking control in these respects from the community and from the state. Some commonwealths, in economic stress, have made new alliances with the church in the support and hence ultimately in the control of education. In some respects the fundamental theory of the American system, as it involves the distinction between state and government, the complete independence of church from both state and government, and the separation of government into three independent and non-interfering branches, executive, legislative, and judicial, is being attacked. Some forces undermining these principles have been at work over a period of years. What the outcome of this tendency will be no one can tell. Time alone will reveal the substantiality of these forces and the permanency of the changes.

Throughout all of these changes from the situation observed in the early colonial period to the modifications of the third decade of the present century there has been an underlying as well as universal recognition of the right of the individual to decide the character of his own education or that of his children. Well in the twentieth century there occurred the Oregon referendum case. The people of Oregon adopted a constitutional amendment forbidding children the right of attending private or church schools during the period of compulsory education, that is until fourteen years of age. But the Supreme Court of the United States set aside this amendment as abridging the fundamental right of the individual as guaranteed by the constitution of the United States. Thus the right of the individual to pursue his own conception of education is preserved. But the right of the church or any other body is preserved only as it in turn expresses the will of the state.

Proposals are now before the legislature of several commonwealths to subsidize from taxation sources certain activities of church schools such as payment for transportation of children. But so far as the writer is aware no violation of the essential fundamental principles has been made. The major aspect of the new situation is that the federal government has interfered in undertaking many educational activities. Most of these involve the conflict of federal versus local government power over education, not the principle of government versus state. For the most part these modifications apply to novel educational situations which have arisen out of the present abnormal conditions. It is too early yet to indulge in any generalization about this development. Of the many tendencies some of them developed long before the present economic disturbances began. When fully developed such modifications would throw the United States among those nations where education is controlled directly by the government. But a long time will be necessary to complete such a development. Even were this development completed, the United States would need to be classified with Australia and New Zealand as partaking of the character of both the Continental type of education under government control and of the English type of individual education.

The defence of this traditional American attitude, involving the separation of state, government, and church in the control of education and the assignment of the control of education to the state or the community, does not deny that recently there have developed serious consequences which call for consideration of the entire education procedure. Standards of conduct and behaviour have been greatly modified. By many these changes are attributed to the very general elimination of the religious element from education. The chief query raised in rebuttal of this charge is, why, then, are there similar changes in regard to moral conduct in those societies where the other conception of education prevails?

It is also recognized that changes in economic and industrial life have produced very great social changes to which education has not yet made adequate adjustment. Occupational education has not kept abreast of changes in industry and in economic life. So there are a vast number of unemployed and even unemployable among the youth who have passed through the traditional educational system. Novel social forces have developed which have great educational significance,

G

rival the school in educational influence, and bid defiance to the conventional educational procedures. These novel forces are all outgrowths of new inventions—the radio, the cinema, and the automobile. It will be admitted that the system of education under direct government control, where decisions of universal application can be put into practice immediately, apparently have a more direct control over and a wider use of these new forms of education than have the more individual systems of the traditional type.

These considerations but indicate that all educational systems face common problems which have not been solved by any one of the systems, and that modern life contains elements which may not yield to the traditional treatment. If this analysis proves to be the true one, then traditional education both in England and in the United States as well as in those of the first type may have to modify its standards and adjust itself to new conditions both to make use of the new technique and to control situations that have not existed hitherto.

These principles which have been discussed are the products of the growth of American democracy. Obviously they are quite different from those produced by the development of democracy in England. The institutions as well as the theory and ideals of democracy are developed everywhere in response to local conditions and novel political forms. These characteristic principles developed through the past may now be modified.

But to date the American system constitutes the one clear example of the distinction between state and government, of the control of education by the state, and not by the government or by the community organized on a religious basis, and of the relegation of the control of religious beliefs and practices to the individual or to the community acting independently of all political organizations. As such it lies midway between the continental European system, where education is controlled directly by the government, and England, where education is controlled largely by local community acting either as church or as local government, or as individuals, or as institutions such as Universities or Public Schools.

To have this system disappear in the stress of the new problems of the twentieth century would be a catastrophe similar to that of the disappearance of the political and economic principles of democracy.

THE STATE AND VOLUNTARY
EFFORT

by

C. R. MORRIS

THE STATE AND VOLUNTARY EFFORT

THE totalitarian states know exactly what they want to produce in their educational systems and give the whole energy of their educational machines to producing it. It is not easy to see what will be the effect of these single-minded efforts in the long run; but in the short run they seem able to produce results which are a triumph for modern organization and which leave the democracies, with their ideas of liberal education, seriously disquieted and in some respects jealous. Disquieted because the education, being directed to a spurious end, seems to us dangerous; jealous because it seems to be so effective in doing what it sets out to do.

Nor can we satisfy ourselves with the easy comfort that education for a circumscribed idea produces results which are easier to see than those effected under the loftier democratic ideal of a liberal education. This is no doubt true; but we know it is not the whole truth. Our ambitious efforts are not only less effective in producing quick results than the more cut and dried enterprise of our totalitarian rivals; they are also less effective than they ought to be, taken for what they are. And we are being driven to inquire into our own education to see what is the matter with it. There are many things of course which the totalitarian philosophy allows, and indeed requires, its educators to do, where democratic faith requires us to do nothing. But are we doing all that we can do; are we doing all that we must do if democracy and freedom are to survive? Many of us feel that we are not merely failing to stimulate in our people a spurious vigour which we can well do without; we are also failing to give scope for the proper encouragement of the natural and healthful vigour which a free people must have if it is to defend its freedom.

Sir Michael Sadler has pointed out that "a strong flavour of individualism" has pervaded the well-known definitions of a liberal education. Much thought has been given to the question of what such an education will do for the man who receives it, but little to the question of what it will enable him to do for the community to which he belongs. Little credit has been given to the community for the cultural influence it has exercised on the liberal education which has been given and received within its borders, and for the sacrifices it has made to maintain the institutions which made it possible. Nor have the needs of the community received much consideration. It has been assumed that whatever creatures are produced by a liberal education can be absorbed with benefit by the community at large. Educators need not consider the nature and needs of the society into which they were turning out their finished pupils; they should simply hitch their wagon to the star of absolutely liberal education and leave it at that. It is not surprising that so many "liberally educated" men became detached from the common lot, unduly fastidious, absorbed in rather selfish study and a little frightened by the rough and tumble of practical life.

Many of these "liberal" theorists were Englishmen. It need not be said that English practice in education has never entirely conformed to this theory. It is commonly accepted that for a good part of the nineteenth century the English schools for the middle and upper classes produced something that was wanted, socially and politically, though not of course all that was wanted. But the theory affected the practice, and in so far as thoughtful people helped to influence the tradition they for the most part pushed it in the direction of the theory. And, what is perhaps more serious, such elements in the practice of education as were not represented in the theory persisted or developed haphazard and without forethought; in so far as the education adapted itself to social conditions and social needs it did so through more or less opportunist adjustment by enterprising practical teachers with a gift for small inventions in the trade and an eye for a situation, whose underlying ideas about social needs and social conditions were those of the club or of the street—the ideas of men who were too busy getting on with the job to feel the need for any deep thought about the nature of society in general. Jowett, for instance, had his own ideas about what was socially, or imperially, wanted and those ideas, since he was a great practical educator, exercised an enormous influence on English education; but his thoughts about the essential nature and needs of human society were neither inspired nor profound. In the realm of fundamental ideas he took from his world, he gave nothing to it. The same is true to a less degree of Arnold. In a word, education was developing itself as a rather competent professionalism, with a good deal of opportunism in meeting situations without real forethought, and covered by a partially spurious ideal of "liberalism."

It is difficult even now for an educational enthusiast who has been brought up in a free country to bear too hardly upon this "liberal" ideal. No doubt it lived in a fool's paradise in thinking that, if you look after the individual, society will look after itself. But the educator ought to keep one eye on the infinite; and there is something noble about a vision which sees no need to compromise with practical social difficulties, but simply asks itself "What was the individual intended to be?" and then tries to turn him into that. This is education in the grand manner; and where its principle is accepted great power falls into the hands of those educators who are looking to the future generation—which at least is better than letting it all rest with those whose whole attention is given to the problem of surviving by hook or by crook until to-morrow, of not being utterly crushed by the wreckage of to-day. Any education which has not more than a touch of this grand manner does not deserve the name, and must prove a delusion to those who trust in it.

But the problems which have not been thought out by the classical definers of a liberal education must be thought out, and soon. The ideal of traditional liberalism does not as it stands command acceptance to-day; and unless it is reborn, its place will be taken everywhere by pseudo-ideals such as the true educator must always disown, since they involve the prostitution of that whose value is infinite by using it as a means to the convenient overcoming of ephemeral difficulties. The defence of democracy calls for a vindication of the common-sense thesis that education can be liberal in every sense that matters without being individualistic to the point of being dangerously anti-social, and that it is possible to serve absolute values without remaining in a fool's paradise about the conditions and needs of actual society.

Some have been tempted to think that the case can be met by simple changes of technique in our educational system. They urge that we turn out pupils who have been given no information about the social and political system in which they will live, and that an appreciation of the finer points of a Greek or English lyric, or an ability to manipulate differential equations, is not a satisfactory substitute for such information. Not unlike those who have set unbounded store by the dissemination among young children of knowledge of the physical facts of sexual reproduction, they fly to the hope that by including some lessons on the social sciences in the curriculum of all our schools they will turn out a generation of young men and women who will have so firm a hold on true values in all the important affairs of life that they will effectively defend democracy—they will be unable to be seduced from the service of free institutions, and will show that vigour and determination in collective action which at present we unhappily associate not with the children of light but with the forces of darkness. Our curriculum has been too narrow, they say, and our teachers have been too academic. Let every boy and girl be taught in the schools to understand the basic social and political problems of their time and country, and let them as far as possible be initiated into these studies by men and women who know something of social and political life at first hand. Then they will be trained to pull their own weight as citizens and militant members of the good society, and apathy, irresponsible fractiousness, and collective inaction will be no more.

It is clear that those who make this point are so far in the right that the curriculum must certainly be broadened in this sense. But it would be a delusion to suppose that such a change would go to the root of the matter and would solve the problem. Even if his attention is directed to the most urgent problems of the day, and even if a Napoleon or a Lenin himself be his mentor, it is impossible to escape the fundamental law that the pupil will only learn what he is capable of learning, what his own experience enables him to learn. The educator who hopes that Etonians or Wykehamists will acquire a juster appreciation of our social system from listening to a William Booth or a Keir Hardie than from being taught by a research sociologist will too often be disappointed. So long as the pupil has experience of no more than one kind of people, he may learn to remember external facts about other kinds of people, but no more. Let us not delude ourselves with *a priori* hopes. No great man is a hero to his valet, said the philosopher, not because the great man is not a great man, but because the valet is a valet. And the crude fact is that so long as a schoolboy remains a schoolboy, he will probably get less insight into the working of parliamentary institutions by listening to a Prime Minister than he will gain from any competent schoolmaster.

What we want in the next generation, and what our present educational system is not giving us in sufficient measure, is vigour; a capacity to live together without losing enthusiasms and to act together with power in attacking vital problems and defending vital values. And in this age when the social conscience is so sensitive, and when there is so acute and troubling an awareness of impending political catastrophe, our education with all its liberality is not producing that vigour. It is clear that something more than a simple extension of the curriculum is required to produce it.

The simple way, of course, to meet the case is the totalitarian way; give to youth a clear and unquestioned objective, which shall as far as possible be a form without content but tricked out to look thoroughly concrete, and use for all it is worth the powerful apparatus which modern science has contributed to the educator's armoury to canalize all the emotional forces in the individual so as to produce collective action in pursuit of that objective. This can be done, and it is being done in some parts of Europe. Educationally there is nothing in principle new about it. It has been done before in Japan; the Jesuits have done it and a hundred others. We perhaps understand in theory a little more than we did how those gifted people who run such "educational" institutions manage to do it; but it is doubtful how far such increased theoretic understanding really affects or assists the practice of the gifted people in question. What modern scientific knowledge has done is vastly to extend the range of action of a few gifted persons. The totalitarians can perhaps do little more—it is hardly possible to do more than has been done in the past—with the relatively small band of *élite*, on which they ultimately rely; but they can do far more, thanks to broadcasting and the Press, with the great mass of the people. This undoubtedly means that a few suitably gifted persons, if they serve anti-democratic, anti-liberal ends, can be far more dangerous to the survival of freedom in the world at large than they have ever been before. Just as the invention of the tank, the armoured car, and the aeroplane has enormously increased the possibilities of controlling the whole population by physical force through a small *élite*, so, to come nearer to the life of the spirit, the development of propaganda has made the many almost defenceless before the few. And hence democracy is challenged in defence of her life to find and cultivate springs of vigour in her free people which shall enable her if necessary to resist the quasi-fanatical energy of totalitarianism.

The trouble is that while a good deal has been known for a long time about the craft of propaganda, very little is still known about the mystery of education. The scrupulous educator knows all about the tricks of the hypnotist, and of other unscrupulous exploiters of human instruments; in many cases he could, if he wished, perform the tricks himself. But except in the very best material he cannot generate as much sheer active efficiency in properly educated persons. And bound as he is to treat all human beings as worthy of a proper education, in so far as he can give it he puts the society in which he serves at a short-run disadvantage as against other communities whose teachers accept a different faith. In his attempts to solve his problem he has sometimes resorted to a training of the free intellect which has too often starved the emotions and paralysed action, and sometimes has cultivated the emotions, still with a respect for the demands of freedom, only to produce a kind of romantic anarchy. And now while he is still attempting to find the true solution, the liberal educator finds that his world bids fair to be brought about his head in ruins through the short-run potency of the methods of rivals who have no respect or care for the mystery of education at all.

But let us return to the main issue. If we could accept totalitarianism, or something like it, we could solve our problem. If the state made up its mind what its citizens were to be taught to believe, what values they were to be taught to have at heart, then a people prepared to move vigorously in the given direction could perhaps be produced—or at least our educators would know how to set to work, even if it meant undoing the effects of generations of free institutions in the past. But if the state may not use its educational system to hypnotize its citizens and stimulate their emotional responses all in one direction, what can the educator do? There seems to be general agreement, in the light of past experience, that it is not enough in these days to cultivate the free intellect and to leave the education of the emotions to look after itself. The schools used to be able to confine their attention to the intellect without harm in an age when a certain stability and uniformity in the life and enthusiasms of the people could be taken for granted. So long as the general direction of a man's life could be taken purely as given, intellectual cultivation could do him little harm and normally did him much good. But in an age when a boy or girl on leaving school or

university is going out into a world in which there is
no strong current of religious, moral, social, or political
orthodoxy—a world of "emancipated" persons who
mostly feel bewildered in their largely unwanted freedom, like sheep without a shepherd—then the whole case
is very different. Then the main problem for the educator
is not to train the intellect as an instrument, and perhaps
to cultivate and liberalize a rough people with the crude
energy and drive of pioneers: his chief task is rather to
help every free man to find for himself a cause to which
he can really devote himself, and meanwhile to help him
to train himself for what will one day be a strenuous
life-endeavour needing all the emotional drive that there
is in human nature.

Some liberal educators still hope that it is possible to
find a technique for doing this without determining the
direction in which the drive shall go; that just as it seems
possible up to a point to train the intellect as an instrument without knowing to what uses it will be put, so
it should prove feasible to develop and keep at high
efficiency a kind of emotional power-unit in the individual, which shall be there to give powerful service when
called upon. But experience seems to belie this hope.
The principle involved is not to-day very widely accepted
in its application to intellectual training; and as applied
to the emotional nature it has perhaps never seemed
very plausible except to a few extreme romantics.

The alternative, if we follow the orthodox political
principles of practical liberalism in England, would be
to allow free play to voluntary associations in stimulating
the active enthusiasms of people, even of young people;
and for the educational system to accept these enthusiasms as given, to come to terms with them and to lend
itself not to their frustration or discouragement, but to
the training of the young for the pursuit of their enthu-

siasms with active efficiency, vigour, and common sense.
This would mean that the educator would not embrace
that negative and spurious liberalism which too often
produces in the pupil merely an excessive detachment
and a total inability to be fired by a generous enthusiasm;
he would rather welcome a sense of vocation where he
found it and would take account of it in the training
of the pupil's mind and character. No doubt this would
mean a certain predestination of the individual; the boy
would put his hand early to a plough and his education
would help to make it unlikely that he would turn back.
But if all went well, he would, in addition to acquiring
an appropriate skill, be accumulating energy and learning
confidence in his own power; and he would be content
in the discovery that it is a clear way to the living of a
full life to co-operate with other like-minded people in
the service of a cause. Moreover, under such conditions
the capacity to make things go well in the educational
scheme would not demand more than human ability;
it would be well within the power of the educators of
to-day to fulfil the task required.

It may appear to some that to take this course would
be to acquiesce in all that matters in the underlying thesis
of the totalitarian state. If it is agreed that the whole
of education should be through and through imbued with
the ideal of training for the service of some end, what
more can the totalitarian himself demand? If the individual is to devote himself body and soul to co-operation
in some movement or group, and education is simply
to enable him to do this more efficiently and thoroughly,
what is there left for the liberal to live for? It will matter
to him very little in that case whether there are many
groups or few, or whether the whole nation is gathered
up into one all-embracing totalitarian movement. As
far as the life of the spirit is concerned, the tyranny of a

small group over the individual can be as deadly as that of a large. In any such society freedom must be dead.

But surely to argue thus would be absurd. There is absolute validity in the liberal claim that the vigour and spontaneity of the individual must not be swamped in the vigour of the group. Any society which does not conform to this principle, whatever its professed aims may be, is in fact defeating the very end which societies exist to serve. But no individual can live in complete and utter solitariness, even of the spirit. In the supposedly individualistic ages of the past, single persons lived much less self-dependent lives than they thought they did, or than some historians have allowed; and no thoughtful person wishes to live without some sense of solidarity with others of his kind. No doubt in the highest type of religious society there seems to be an almost complete absence of group interference in the terrestrial activities of members of the society. The solidarity is the solidarity of a communion of saints or of a city of God, not of a regiment of soldiers. But the society is there, and the sense of communion it gives; and the life of the spirit cannot be lived without it.

The real question is not whether there are to be societies and communions, but what kind of societies and communions there are to be. Where there is freedom there will always be some societies which leave to their members the fullest individual enterprise and spontaneity of which human beings are capable. There will also be many associations and organizations where members need a closer orthodoxy and a tighter discipline. In the totalitarian state there is only one organization with a full orthodoxy and an almost infinite discipline. In our revulsion against this extreme, we must not forget that real isolation from others is not spiritual life but spiritual death; and that freedom to work with others

H

in a self-chosen cause is the most priceless freedom man
can have. This does not mean that every man who is
spiritually alive must be enrolled in the membership of
some social or political organization, and must give three
evenings a week to fighting its good fight. But it does
mean that the man who does not feel some sense of
solidarity and spiritual alliance with some other people
or groups of people is spiritually lost.

Surely the ideal society is not one in which individuals
are as far as possible so completely insulated from one
another that each can manifest a pure and unadulterated
activity of his own, but one in which societies and associations are allowed to find their own level, and so can
have a fair chance really to satisfy the needs of their
members. Not all such societies will do battle for some
tangible end or promulgate some clearly articulated
doctrine; and the bonds which maintain the unity of
some will be light as compared with those of others.
But the educator who has the needs of the good society
in mind will wish to favour the growth of particular
solidarities where he can; since it is out of such solidarities that there springs effective and persistent action
and vigorous living.

The totalitarian has partially recognized this truth,
only he has not scrupled to drive the whole nation into
one vast solidarity—the solidarity of the race or nation.
Nothing could be further from the ideal of allowing
societies and groups to find their own level; nothing
would be less like the form of society outlined above.
But where totalitarianism has gone wrong in the eyes
of the liberal is not in denying that man is in spirit a
completely isolated individual, not in recognizing that
ultimately man must live in some association with his
fellows, but in claiming to merge every individual life
into one great association, whose ends and means are

through and through beyond the control of the individual will. This compulsory driving of everyone into one rigidly organized group, which controls him body and soul, means the death of any true freedom. It is this which is the real enemy of the spirit of liberalism, and which must be fought to the end.

The encouragement of association and of co-operative acting and living under free conditions is an entirely different matter, and as supporters of the liberal ideal, we need not regret it or apologize for it. The fact that there are in the community zealots of many kinds, and not only of one kind, in itself makes a great deal of difference to the education in each kind. Under these circumstances we have to train ourselves to work for our appointed end within a society in which other groups of people are working for other ends. We shall not train ourselves as if we could take it for granted that our own group was the only pebble on the beach; we shall have to respect the rights of other groups. And though our zealots will none the less have a purpose in life and will be prepared to make the greatest sacrifices for it, it will be part of their purpose that they should achieve their end within a free society. And this will affect the whole education through and through. The whole training of a zealot for a free association within a free society will be utterly different from the training of a totalitarian zealot. And yet there is no reason why the training of the former should leave him less vigorous or less full of missionary fire than the latter; though no doubt his proper education is a more difficult thing to achieve.

But what of the state? Will not this training of sectional zealots, breathing fire each for his own cause, make of the community as a whole nothing but a bear garden? Shall we have got rid of our rather vigourless apathy only to tear society apart with the internecine struggles of warring groups? I think not. In educational matters we must show a little faith; and a little faith in this direction is not ill-grounded. Even in these chaotic times since the War experience seems to have shown that the unity of our national groupings takes a good deal of tearing asunder; and we seem to be faced by the prospect of a world in which the state of international affairs will make us all take it for granted for many generations to come that the interests and security of our nation must come first. Moreover, it seems that the great educational systems to-day have the secret of implanting an implicit loyalty to the nation, an implicit conviction, which will come to the surface in appropriate circumstances, that the interests of the nation must be paramount. Indeed, the fear is that, even outside the totalitarian states, the power of our education in this direction is not too weak but too strong. The very real forces which might have united international groups—Roman Catholics, for instance, or the workers of the world—and induced them to break up nationalisms, have so far proved almost powerless against our existing education. We need not therefore allow ourselves to become the prey to an unnecessary hysterical fear that we shall inevitably swing to an opposite extreme with sudden violence. All our history is against it. Our education has the secret of implanting this implicit loyalty to the nation; and let us recognize this fact and use it for what it is worth. It is better for the loyalty to be implicit. So long as it remains so there is far less danger of its being bound up with some static idea—such as Aryanism —or worse still of being cast into the mould of loyalty to a particular person or government than is the case with an explicit loyalty, carefully fostered and inflamed with nation-wide song and dance. And yet in a vigorous people it is strong enough and reliable enough, when brought to the surface by an appropriate emergency, to meet every need.

In a vigorous people, the trouble is that in our anxiety to guard freedom, and liberalism in education, we have let the methods of our schools and universities enervate and emasculate our youth as far as their potency for social action is concerned. We have been afraid of encouraging zealotry in particular groups, fearing both for freedom and for national unity. This was surely a mistake. A vigorous people will transfer the vigour of its ordinary living to its defence of national values when it is required to turn and defend them. On the other hand a people that is disillusioned and frustrated in its ordinary living will keep its disillusionment and frustration in all spheres and at all times. Let us then be always in our education inspired by the guiding notion that every pupil is being trained to use to the full his powers as a zealot for something. There need be no derogation in principle from freedom. A man or a boy is not the less free because we remind him that if his education is to be properly planned he must put his hand to some plough. If, as in the totalitarian states, only one plough is offered him, then any talk of liberty is indeed an illusion. But no thoughtful man asks for freedom to be nothing and to do nothing. Yet in educating we have perhaps behaved as if men were like that, or the next thing to that—that is, unwilling or perhaps unable to make up their minds. We have in effect said to our pupils, "Never mind, do not worry to commit yourselves yet; take your time; and in the meantime we will get on with training your capacities so that when you do make up your mind when you do give yourself entirely to the service of some cause, you will find all your faculties and abilities developed, and you will have all the power of which you are capable immediately available for that service!" All this we have done in the service of liberalism in education, and we have waited for experience to teach us that such an education will not do. We ought perhaps to have known it all along.

And yet it was a natural mistake to make. It was inevitable that the state should accept the responsibility for educating its citizens, and it has certainly done so once and for all. About that there can be no going back. And granted that a state accepted the liberal principle of tolerance, of respect for the freedom of the spirit, what was it to do? If it must decline to exploit its powerful position as educator to force its young citizens into a spiritual mould determined by itself, what could it do except look for an education which would train mere abilities, without giving any bias towards any one direction rather than any other for their exercise? And having imposed this self-denying ordinance upon itself, what more natural than that it should use its position to push churches and other groups in the same direction, so far as they would allow themselves to be pushed. Nor need we accuse the state too vehemently of being a dog in the manger. It is rather that it accepted this pseudo-liberal idea as an ideal and made itself its prophet.

Since we are now satisfied from experience that what this idea enjoins us to do undoubtedly turns out ill, we may well set ourselves to do some thinking which we ought to have done before. Let us see whether the state cannot lend its educational system for the training of zealots of all sorts and kinds, confident that the state itself will ultimately reap all necessary benefit—that the vigour and power which is given in ordinary living to the service of other causes will return home to a unified defence of the state when a true need arises. Let us have the courage of our convictions and show a little faith. Let us give up the notion that liberal training must be training for nothing in particular. If a group of people want to devote themselves to some cause, let us give up talking about detachment and impartiality and give them the services of our educational system to enable them to equip themselves for their task and learn to do it well and truly. If we care to look at the facts, we can assure ourselves that we dare go a long way in this direction without much risk. With the help of history and tradition our educators, almost without noticing it, drive home into the young a deep sense of national unity which has power and to spare for resisting disruption; and we live in a world in which this sense of national unity is everywhere too strong, not too weak. We may safely have the courage to use our schools and universities to develop vigour rather than to frustrate it, even though the ends which that vigour will be used to serve may be "sectional" in times of ordinary living. We can rely on that vigour coming home to the service of the nation at any time when nationalism ought to be served.

This will seem to many to be an almost unbelievably idealistic and impractical suggestion, such as would come only from one who has lived his life in the cloistered seclusion of a British university. And to those who think thus it will not be easy to find a convincing reply. But it is by no means certain that they think rightly. Claiming to read correctly the signs of the times, they argue that freedom for zealotry will eventually bring into existence zealots who will destroy the freedom. Those who believe in the abolition of free institutions, they say, will use the licence given to them to promulgate their subversive views, until they become strong enough to liquidate the free institutions which gave them their chance. They will exploit the very virtues of the democrat for his own destruction, and when he falls the victim of his own high-mindedness they will despise him for an innocent and idealistic fool.

This is not the place to embark upon a long argument on this point, though it would raise questions both of method and of value which are of fundamental importance. But it is necessary to say enough to show that the issue is not shirked. There is clearly no reason of principle why the liberal should allow those who believe in the destruction of free institutions to drill and arm themselves and to organize a powerful fighting machine. It is freedom of speech and freedom of association which he is pledged to defend. No doubt, too, democracy is liable to the inherent disease of indecision and weakness of will in the handling of illiberal minorities until it is too late. But no great height can be reached without risk, and no man or society is without human weaknesses. These difficulties must be courageously faced and shown to be capable of being overcome. No nation which has known anything at all of the life of freedom has been induced to turn from it except in a time of the extremest despair; and no nation which has really got to know and love such a life in its very bones has yet been induced to turn from it at all.

Above all, wherever there is a chance of a reasonably cool and calm appeal to reason, it has yet to be shown that free institutions have anything to fear. No one would welcome practical totalitarianism if it dropped out of a clear sky. The ideal of personal freedom is a noble ideal, worth taking risks for. If once it could be dissociated from the charge of normally leading to the sort of dilatory government which is a stronghold for the indiscriminate defence of the *status quo*, it would stand forth without challenge in the eyes of all as the noblest social ideal there is—far more satisfying than any materialistic aim whatever, however altruistic or equalitarian it may be. It is an ideal that owes a great deal to Christianity, and it must command the allegiance of any

Christian, if once he can be satisfied that it is practical politics. And it is on this ground that it must stand. Unless we have the faith and courage to maintain it there, we shall be unworthy defenders, because it will not be free institutions that we are defending.

In the end freedom will only be loved and defended by those who use it. The man who, though he is free to work for any cause he wills, does not in practice care for anything sufficiently to work for it with any enthusiasm, will at a pinch prove but a poor champion of a liberty which has never really meant anything to him. The best thing our educational system can do to defend democracy is to turn out men and women who really enjoy and care for that vigorous individual life and work which would not be allowed to them under a totalitarian system. And this is what at present our democratic schools and universities are largely failing to do.

It is not easy to see what practical conclusions should be drawn from these principles, and it would be foolish here to attempt to give more than tentative suggestions. One thing, however, is certain; we should not conclude that education, in any part of it, should cease to be the care of the state. The state has the greatest duty to educate, and it is itself the chief beneficiary when that duty is performed. Again, it seems to be almost certain that we should not conclude that all schools should be sectional schools, each training pupils of one kind to serve one purpose in life. Europe is not likely at this date to give up the idea of a "university"; and the same principles apply not only to the instruction of those of maturer years but to education at any stage. Education in a segregated order may gain something in intensity of vocation;

but it loses more in appreciation and understanding of human nature, apart from the serious practical disadvantage of missing an opportunity for full acclimatization to the ethos of the particular society in which the pupils will have to serve. It seems to be the least that the state may reasonably demand, that every school and college should be sufficiently broadly based as regards the origins from which its members spring that every boy and girl in the course of the ordinary living of school life may acquire a natural sensitivity to the whole range of types and interests that are to be found within the community. Experience seems to show conclusively that where this is not so, nothing can repair the harm both of omission and commission that results; no arrangement of curriculum, no teaching technique can give to the child or young man what he should be breathing in with every breath that he draws in his school life. To fail to give to children these conditions is to deceive them vitally during their impressionable years about the nature of the world in which they will have to live.

If this is accepted, it is clear that it is very difficult to see how we are in practice to apply the general principles at which we have arrived above. If we are not to encourage the isolation of people of a particular kind or with a particular vocation, how are we to see to it that education shall encourage and empower, rather than . discourage and frustrate, particular enthusiasms and particular vocations?

Prima facie there seem to be two kinds of experience above all upon which it is worth while to reflect in trying to find out what is and what is not practicable within the limits of a liberal system—the experience of our universities and the contribution to national education of our system of non-provided schools.

Let us consider these in the other order. At first sight

it might seem that the natural way of trying to apply the principles we have advocated would be to multiply the provision of non-provided schools, following the main lines of such development in the past. In this way it might seem that voluntary associations of a suitable character could make their contribution to the spiritual vitality of the youth of the nation by arranging for the education together of those who have some common ideal or faith, and thereby promoting that solidarity and confident consciousness of common purpose which can make the average individual show so much more heroism and determination than he could ever do if he stood alone. But on reflection it is clear that the non-provided school does not offer the solution to this particular problem.

In the first place it must be clearly emphasized that anything like the existing establishment of non-provided schools in England does not cover what is to-day the vital ground. To-day the living issues are different from what they were before the War. It must be remembered that we are concerned primarily not with those questions differences of opinion about which are ultimately the most important *sub specie aeternitatis*, but with those where differences are felt in the community at large to be vital and fundamental. It is here that the "liberal" system, as we have experienced it, so effectively operates to cause the issues to be shirked and to prevent any teacher from giving real light and leading or from promoting any full-blooded and well-directed enthusiasm. To-day, owing to the rapidly growing sensitiveness of the public mind to social and political evils, the thing that really stirs passions in religious teaching, as in history teaching, is the bearing of what is taught on man's whole attitude to social evils and to the problems of war and international justice. Has Christianity a social teaching and a teaching about war? Or is true Christian doctrine teachable in terms which exhibit it as having no clear bearing on these issues, so that the individual must think out its application for himself? Or, if Christianity has a teaching on these points, what is it? Again, where exactly does legitimate defence of the Christian faith against the anti-Christianism of Bolshevism become in effect preaching against the legitimate aspirations of the working-class movement? And so on. These are all questions upon which the reasonable man will expect to find serious differences of opinion, and these are the questions which stir passionate emotions in the community; these in a word are the issues upon which "liberal" principles are most sure to drive us into a shirking of the issues during the years of education and a consequent atrophy in the real life of the spirit. Any member of an Education Committee knows that in these days for every one protest against a piece of teaching on a point of "pure" doctrine or "pure" ethics, there are ten against religious or historical teaching which appears to have clear implications about a social issue or about the questions of war. We are not a nation of very good Christians; but we are a Christian-minded people. Ideologically we are all within the Christian fold, and we pose our issues and promulgate our conclusions in Christian terms. It is *within* our religious education that our living issues arise to-day, not in a battle between Christianity and atheism, or Christianity and anything else. What is more, they do not lie between confession and confession, but *within* the religious teaching of the various confessions.

Thus the alignment of the establishment of the confessional non-provided schools does not correspond to what from our point of view are the vital matters of the day. But this is not all. It seems, to say the least of it, doubtful whether any re-alignment would meet the situation—that is, whether any expedient of this general kind can satisfactorily meet the situation. Against the non-provided school as such I have nothing to say. The arguments in favour of allowing its existence under certain conditions and for certain purposes are no doubt strong. But it seems unthinkable that the establishment of such schools could be developed to meet the particular needs with which we are here concerned. This whole expedient is surely admissible only where the conditions in the community as regards relevant matters of faith allow the principle involved to be restricted in its application within very moderate limits. It is one thing to have chains of non-provided schools under the aegis of four or five confessions; it would be quite another to allow them to grow up under the auspices of any body or association which was enthusiastic enough to promulgate particular views about the proper education of youth. In actual practice, if such associations had to back their enthusiasms by raising substantial sums of money in order to pay a considerable proportion of the cost of the schools, few of them would seriously enter the field and the problem would not be met; if on the other hand the state showed itself so favourable to non-provided schools that it bore almost the whole of their cost, the various voluntary bodies would leap into the field and would surely produce chaos. Thus it seems difficult to believe either that the system of non-provided schools as at present existing does much to mitigate the essential weaknesses of the "liberal" tradition in education, or that an extension of the application of the principle could do much more.

We may now turn to consider the other kind of experience which was mentioned above as worth examining for our purpose. Do the methods of our universities suggest lines along which a solution of our problem may be sought in our schools?

Many critics will no doubt hold that our universities are subject to the same paralysis as infects all modern "liberal" education at all its stages; that here, too, is the same fear of allowing anyone, whether professor or student, to develop any strong conviction which is not shared by everyone else in the community, or to train himself for an effective life of service of any particular ideal. Unfortunately there is too much evidence in support of this view. But it may fairly be claimed that, even within the limits of principles and expedients well established in experience, the outlook in liberal universities is not without hope. In the case of young men and women of university age it is not beyond the capacity of the liberal educator's art to encourage a real sense of vocation and a real spiritual vigour without incurring much danger of falling into the totalitarian pit of propaganda, or anything like it—and this without recourse to the expedient of sectarian colleges. At university age it is perhaps possible to approach the liberal ideal of providing the young with the equipment, and of developing in them the determination, to go ahead with energy along their own road without dictating to them what that road shall be. Even while the university remains a true university, in the fullest and most liberal sense of the word, much can be done to arrest that spiritual vigourlessness which, if we are right, has too generally been the product of the conscientious application in educational practice of liberal principles.

This is partly because in university education at its best more use can be made of personal contact in the proper sense—that is, real unrestricted intercourse and communion between individual and individual; and partly because the greater maturity of the students makes it possible to allow far more freedom to university teachers than is possible with those who teach young children—

not at ?Manchester University unfortunately

freedom to express their own faiths, live their lives in the
service of their own ideals, and thereby show themselves to
be persons of strong conviction and vigour in the service
of their convictions—and so to influence their pupils by
example. All this is recognized in practice. Very few
people are disquieted when they find the universities
turning out zealots of unorthodox views, and on the
whole the universities are showing some capacity to
survive and even encourage a constantly rising tem-
perature in student life, a constant tendency for under-
graduates to be infected with a growing impatience to
get to work in the world at large for the promotion of
some cause which they hold to be good. If this is a good
thing the universities have a long way to go before they
will realize their full potentialities; but at least it is clear
that in this sphere something can be done. The universities can, if they wish, contribute to the task of educating
a strenuous youth without violating anything essential
in liberal principles.

The same secret can be extended to adult education,
and here too the state has already shown itself willing
to go a long way. Working-class adult education in
England has been rendered possible only by the willingness of the state to provide classes for a particular section
of the community on terms which in many essentials
were laid down by that section itself. Many of the classes
are exclusively drawn from members of the working-
class movement, which has a considerable solidarity of
outlook and sentiment; students are interested in working-
class problems and are normally sturdily enthusiastic to
promote the future welfare of working people. But the
state has not objected to this; it has insisted that the
teaching should be non-political and non-sectarian, but
with those reservations it has come forward to provide
the education that is asked for, recognizing with grati-

fication that such education enables the students to pursue their own particular purposes with greater effectiveness and sense of proportion. On the whole it may fairly be claimed that the preservation of liberal standards in working-class adult education has not been accompanied by any growth of spiritual paralysis in the promotion of working-class aims, but has contributed considerably to the effectiveness and common sense with which those aims have been pursued.

This has no doubt been rendered possible only by the protection of a liberal university tradition; like university teachers, adult education tutors have been allowed considerable freedom both in their teaching and in their self-devotion to causes in their private lives. There has been little or no reason for thinking this freedom to have any dangerous or detrimental effects from the point of view of sound education or of national unity; and on the side of credit it has done much to acquit adult education of the charge that it operates to paralyse the public will and to produce a listless and apathetic society.

Unfortunately only a small proportion of the community are, or are likely to be, affected directly by university or even by adult education. University education, as we know it in the great universities of Europe, has set before itself a special task, and it demands special aptitudes and interests in the students; and the universities could not extend themselves so as to receive a really large proportion of members of the community without radically changing their aims and methods. To a large extent adult education in England has taken on the same character; it aims not at the mere dissemination of information but at providing a real education, in a fairly ambitious sense of the word. It is not of course uniformly successful in achieving its aims any more than the universities are uniformly successful; but it has met with a

considerable measure of success, and in doing so it has
shown fairly conclusively that, so long as it aims so high,
it cannot expect to touch more than a small proportion
of the population. It can achieve a great deal in the
direction of leavening public opinion, but it cannot
directly and personally touch more than a very small
number of the members of the community. What it does
can only be done for students who have reached an adult
age, and so long as it sticks to the hard road of education,
avoiding the primrose path of propaganda, only a few
adults will give it a chance to do what it can do. We
must reconcile ourselves to the fact that the great majority
of people, when they leave school, pass for ever beyond
the reach of all formal educational influences. What the
educational system does for them must be done in the
schools or not at all.

In the school it is inevitable that the liberal system
should be at a grave disadvantage. If it were desired that
children should be indoctrinated with some particular
scheme of ideas and values, then as Plato and other
totalitarian educationists have seen the younger they are
when the process is begun the better. But if they are to
be encouraged to grow up "free," the educationist must
tie his hands far more restrictively than he need do with
persons of maturer judgment. The sensitivity of youth
to pedagogic tricks is so extreme and so well known
that it is not surprising that a liberal public should be
extremely alert on the lookout for any sign of undue
influence or propaganda; and this means that in all the
humaner subjects the educational fire must inevitably be
damped down all the time. This is a serious matter, as
we have seen; the jealous fear of "undue influence"
encroaches further and further on the subjects in the
curriculum as the public conscience becomes more sensitive and raw. In England we have not yet extended

I

our suspicions to the teaching of arithmetic or ortho-
graphy, but it is becoming increasingly difficult for the
teacher to escape criticism with any teaching of moral
or spiritual import. And the signs are that the educators
themselves are on the run in this matter; instead of
standing up to public opinion and helping it to learn
not to be silly, they too often earnestly anticipate causes
of offence and make the content of their teaching more
conscientiously characterless than ever.

The first necessity is undoubtedly for each of us, and
we may hope for public opinion, to gain some sense of
proportion. We might well show a little less fear of
allowing our teachers to show their own convictions; we
might remember that the immensely varied influences
of the homes are brought to bear on children with as
much force and persistence as the influence of the schools,
and also that even in school each child is after all affected
by more than one teacher. Both the teaching profession
and educational committees ought to stand up to ill-
grounded fears in the public mind far more than they do.

Then it should also be remembered that as the educational system improves the genuine difficulties in the way
of fair-minded education rapidly diminish. As classes get
smaller, personal contact between teacher and individual
pupils can become a constant reality instead of an imprac-
ticable ideal, and the emotional response of the class can
be less mass-produced. The enthusiasm of pupils can be
encouraged along their own lines, instead of there being
a necessity to create artificially a hearty mob-emotion
for the sake of keeping order and maintaining "interest."
When teachers can spare more time and energy for
conference with parents, the latter will be able to think
more effectively about their children's education and the
schools will be less handicapped by the need to keep step
with the demands of ignorant public criticism. Above

all when the average age of school leaving is higher the situation will improve by leaps and bounds. Every year gained after fourteen is of enormous importance; by sixteen it is possible to accustom the child to deal with general ideas and to set him upon the right road in learning to think. In the respects with which we are concerned, there is no doubt an enormous difference between the mind of the young undergraduate of eighteen and that of the schoolboy of sixteen; but it is far less than the gap which divides the school-leaving child of fourteen from his more favoured brother of sixteen. The interest of the latter can be started in subjects which are entirely beyond the range of the former, and invaluable guidance can be given in the early stages; the really vital point is that education can, if only for a few brief months, proceed side by side with the birth and growth of real enthusiasms of a type which may well go on developing into adult life. This is no doubt not worth much unless the individual can be given a reasonable chance to go his own way; but where this is possible, at least a start can be made in the highest stage of education.

Finally, the whole problem will be rendered progressively easier if and when the bitterness of feeling between social classes comes to die down. The fear of undue influence does not really emasculate a liberal educational system unless the matters with regard to which the influence is or may be exerted involve deep and bitter feeling in the community. We do not very much like propaganda in regard to affairs which we consider of small importance, but we can easily show philosophic detachment in expressing our dislike in such cases, and we shall not ordinarily be led to hasty or exaggerated action to prevent it. We have already seen that fears and jealousies based upon religious sectarianism are to-day

nothing like as pervasive or as potent as they used to be.
But an extreme sensitiveness on social matters has taken
their place. When the worst causes of this are removed,
we may reasonably hope that the fear of propaganda
in free societies will sink back into due proportions, and
liberal systems of education will lose their chief weakness.
This happy state of affairs can itself be effectively pro-
moted only by a sound education.

The conclusion of these very insufficient reflections is
that where, as in free societies, the state itself scruples
to provide a full-blooded spiritual content to the education it offers, thereby turning that education into no more
than state-controlled propaganda, the only vital alternative is to welcome the contribution that can be made
by voluntary associations. The educational system must
at all costs learn, not to discourage and frustrate these,
but to adapt itself to them and to train the youth to
use all their abilities in the life of such associations. What
is required is not a change of structure, nor even primarily
a change of machinery in the system, but a slight though
important change of emphasis. So long as associations
are free, free to die as well as to come into being, and
so long as there are many of them and not only one,
it is just a narrow and misguided distortion of liberalism
which rejects them. And as for the apprehension that
the encouragement of zealotry must be but the beginning
of the end, since it acts almost as an invitation to the
enemies of liberty to gird themselves for the fight in which
they will eventually destroy it, we must find the courage
to cast such fears behind us; courageous free institutions
will be worth defending and will not easily be suppressed,
but a semi-liberalism which has not the confidence to

be either one thing or the other will commend itself to nobody.

Free associations will exercise their main effect directly through their appeals to and calls upon adults; but indirectly they will affect the schools and the whole educational structure, in that these will be designed to train appropriately a generation which will live out its life in a community of free associations. Wherever the fire of voluntarism dies, the state will make a desperate effort to save itself by turning totalitarian. The education of a people that is to remain free must be securely based upon voluntary effort.

PART II

THE CRISIS IN CHRISTIAN EDUCATION

by

J. W. D. SMITH

THE CRISIS IN CHRISTIAN EDUCATION

I

IT is significant that *Christian* education should require separate discussion in a volume of this character. European education had its roots in the Church of the Middle Ages and our educational tradition is a Christian one. In spite of diversity of origin or educational objective the universities and schools of Europe retained for centuries the impress of their heritage. There were two basic elements in that heritage which were universally assumed. Man was recognized as a spiritual being with an eternal destiny. He was made by God for life with God. From that fact it followed that man's earthly life only found its meaning and fulfilment in obedience to the moral and spiritual demands of his Christian vocation. God was recognized as the source and ground of all existence, and the ultimate loyalty of man's soul was to Him and to Him only. While these assumptions continued to be a living influence in education there could be no necessity for discussing Christian education as such.

To-day we are faced with the fact that these two assumptions are repudiated openly or implicitly throughout large areas of Europe. In totalitarian countries no loyalty is recognized which transcends loyalty to the current political ideal, and education in Russia is avowedly on an atheistic basis. These facts naturally arrest our attention, but they are merely symptoms of a movement which has affected European civilization as a whole. European thought and life has moved away from its former Christian basis to a degree which we are only now beginning to realize. The change has not been expressed so much in a conscious repudiation of the Christian view as in a gradual loss of living interest in it. Men's thoughts have been turned more and more toward the world of nature and the absorbing interests of temporal life. A new type of civilization has been emerging in which man was regarded, in practice if not at first in theory, as an economic unit or biological entity rather than as a spiritual being made for eternal life with God. During the same period the Christian world-view which unified the thought and experience of medieval Europe suffered successive shocks with the advance of modern science and the old religious certainties were shaken. Christianity retained the traditional allegiance of large numbers of men and women. Religious revivals filled that allegiance with new meaning for many. Nevertheless the processes of decay were not finally arrested. Religious thought and practice became more and more isolated from the main stream of modern life. Thus the way was prepared for that strange blend of Christian ethics with the metaphysics of naturalism which goes by the name of scientific humanism.

The extent to which this process has developed varies in different countries, and its effect is not always clearly recognized. In Britain, for example, the Church still retains a position in public life which conceals the extent to which her hold on the community has weakened, and there is a strong traditional allegiance to Christian values which may create a false impression of the strength of Christian belief. A further source of confusion lies in the fact that the forces of modern life are not essentially anti-Christian. In some respects they are profoundly Christian in spirit. Scientific knowledge brings emancipation to the mind and the methods of science provide a mighty instrument for the refashioning of social life. Industrialism has an ugly sound in modern ears, but it contains untold possibilities for the enrichment of human life if it is properly controlled. And the new doctrines of social life which fill men's thoughts contain germs of truth which we dare not ignore. These forces which are shaping a new culture are not consciously opposed to Christianity, but their fatal weakness is that they are un-Christian. They do not so much deny the reality of God and the spiritual destiny of man as ignore it. Their implicit philosophy is naturalism. To a very great extent naturalism or secularism has become the unacknowledged creed of the educated man.

It is true that the influence of Christian ethics has survived. It may even be claimed with justice that the last few decades have seen the emergence of a keener sense of social justice, a finer ideal of marriage and family life, and a new appreciation of the rights of individual personality. Christians have sometimes played the part of reactionary opponents upholding traditional views and the apostles of humanism have often been the prophets of this moral progress. But their gospel is a late flowering of the Christian ethics and for them the plant has lost its roots in the eternal world. Without these roots it is doomed. It is impossible to combine the ethics of Christianity with the metaphysics of naturalism. An unconditional moral demand can only be laid upon us by a Reality which is unconditioned. Men may set up false Absolutes like the state or they may regard all morality as relative, but they cannot give up God and retain an unconditional allegiance to Christian values. Scientific humanism is an uneasy compromise which cannot last. When the belief in man's spiritual nature and destiny is weakened the logic of the process leads inevitably to a deliberate repudiation of Christian ethics such as we see in Germany to-day.

II

This situation has an important bearing on Christian education. How can religious education be effective within a community which is not itself religious? The subtle forces of community life shape the mind and character of its members far more powerfully than verbal teaching can do. Children growing up in a community unconsciously absorb its traditions, and the prevailing values and beliefs of the community mould their life and conduct. Every individual is a member of several such communities by the time he reaches maturity, and the values embodied in the life of these different groups will often be at variance with one another. Yet beneath these differences all such communities tend to bear the mark of a wider culture in which they share. There are certain features common to any one age which permeate the thought and life of every community comprising it. Herein lies the root cause of the present crisis in Christian education. It is being undertaken within a community which is largely secular.

In the modern community Christian education is primarily the function of the Church. But the Church's members also belong to other communities and are subject to other influences. Provision for religious teaching is quite inadequate, therefore, unless there is clear recognition of the nature and extent of those deeper influences to which everyone is subject. Christian education is likely to be effective, humanly speaking, in two sets of circumstances. If the community life of the Church is strongly marked and the loyalty of its members well developed its educational influence may be profound in spite of contrary influences from other sources. Christian education in tropical Africa takes place in a community which is demonstrably different, in belief

and conduct, from the small Christian groups responsible
for that education. So, too, the early Christian Church
witnessed to a faith and life radically distinct from the
life around it, and it nurtured men and women who
"turned the world upside down." The very contrast may
be a source of strength by intensifying the community
life of the Christians. On the other hand educational
influences of a Christian character will be powerful,
apart altogether from the special contribution of the
Church, in so far as the basic assumptions of the
Christian heritage permeate the general cultural life of
the age.

Neither of these conditions is effectively fulfilled in the
modern world. The Church in Western lands lacks a
distinctive witness which marks its members off from the
life around them. Christians do not commonly feel themselves to be bound closely in common allegiance to a
faith and a way of life which contrasts sharply with those
of the community as a whole. Christian people are deeply
immersed in the life of the community. They are influenced
by its intellectual outlook and social standards. They
participate freely in its practical activities. They are not
conscious of that separateness from the life around them
which marks off the Church of the first century or the
Communist cell to-day. Nor can it be said that the
absence of that sense of separateness is due to a conquest
of the world by the Church. We have noted the fact that
Western civilization has moved steadily away from the
Christian conception of man's nature and destiny during
recent centuries. As a result the educational influences
of the modern community, whether exercised through
its schools or by the unconscious processes of community
life, are predominantly secular. The existence of this
divergence between the Christian faith and the fundae
mental assumptions underlying modern life is a grav-

obstacle to effective Christian education and the danger is greater because it is so seldom recognized.

Of course there always has been and always must be conflict between the Christian faith and the life of the world. It would be false to suggest that European civilization was ever more than very imperfectly Christianized. In some directions there is a more sensitive Christian conscience within that civilization to-day than there ever has been. The real change lies in the fact that the fundamental Christian assumptions about the nature and destiny of man are being openly repudiated or silently ignored and, where that is true, allegiance to Christian values cannot be expected to flourish indefinitely. And the weakness of the Church's position is that this divergence between modern secular culture and the Christian faith has not yet called forth an adequate and distinctive Christian witness. There certainly are points of tension between the Church and the life around it, but the tension seems often to arise at the wrong points.

The creative influence of Christ's life and example must always be at war with the inertia of man's nature and with the pressure of current social custom. The Church does not exist to create a social Utopia nor can it ally itself with political or social groups. But it should act as a ferment within the life of society, cleansing and re-creating the social and economic fabric by the proclamation of Christian values and by the thought and life of its members. This demands a high standard of spiritual sensitiveness, for the pressure of current standards is subtle and persistent. The prophetic note is constantly in danger of being stifled by the weight of tradition and the Church is apt to respond too slowly to the ethical implications of social and industrial changes. The Communist attack on religion focuses on this weakness. It is the opiate of the

people. Instead of working for the realization of Christ's
teaching on earth the Churches have taught men to look
to a future life for the fulfilment of their hopes and ideals.
And the attack though crude is not unjustified. Communism could never have attained its present influence
if the Christian Church as a whole had been sensitive
to the evils of the industrial revolution. But Communist
writers and other social prophets who attack or ignore
religion are mostly preaching a biological ethic which
pays little heed to man's spiritual nature. By so doing
they are destroying the essential foundations of the society
they hope to build. A truly creative Christian community
would find itself deeply critical of the present state of
society yet sharply aware of the shallow philosophy of
many of the popular social reformers. Unfortunately the
Church too often seems to the outsider to come into
conflict with modern social trends on questions like
Sunday games or cinemas and divorce laws, while failing
to appreciate the more fundamental issues raised by the
ethical consequences of nineteenth century individualism.

There must always be tension too on the intellectual
plane. There is a natural tension between the spectator
attitude characteristic of science or philosophy and the
religious attitude. The first is critical and inquiring while
the second is an attitude of worship and acceptance. God
is an object of devotion to the saint, but a subject of
discussion for the philosopher. These two attitudes are
not necessarily contradictory. Both should play their part
in a healthy religious life and the tension between them,
when consciously accepted, will be fruitful intellectually
and spiritually. Unfortunately the Church to-day seems
to many to have created an unnecessary conflict in
the minds of its members by failing to welcome
and assimilate the vast store of new knowledge with
which modern science has enriched our lives. She

seems hesitant and suspicious in her attitude towards the newer sciences of personality and of social relationships. She does not seem conscious of the profound spiritual significance of modern psychology's contribution towards the cure of souls. She seems so far out of touch with the intellectual and spiritual life around her that many of the most sensitive educated men and women of our day fail to find expression for their religious needs and aspirations in her services of worship.

At the same time the Church seems to be insufficiently aware of the real point at which a serious divergence exists between the thought of the age and the faith of the Church. There is no need to defend the faith against modern knowledge. The Christian faith needs no such defence. The real danger which threatens it to-day lies rather in a spiritual malady which affects the whole of modern culture. For four or five hundred years men's interests and energy have been turned persistently towards the world of nature and of human affairs. The progress of science and the growth of industrialism have proved so absorbing that the religious life of man has lost depth and vitality. And the Church herself has shared in this decay of spiritual life. The spiritual world has become so unreal that the best-known religious movement of our day has almost reduced religion to a psychological technique in which God is irrelevant. God has passed out of our lives and we are so steeped in a humanistic culture that we have hardly grasped our loss.

The picture is deliberately exaggerated. If it be even partially true it reveals clearly the obstacles to effective Christian education on the part of the Church. These obstacles are twofold. The Church has been slow to adjust herself to the ethical implications of modern social and industrial developments. Christian ethics is still widely confused with the moral codes of nineteenth century individualism, while those who are sensitive to the social and international issues of the age are deeply divided regarding the true Christian attitude towards them. Thus the Church seems to have no distinctive ethical contribution to modern life and where tension arises it seems often to arise at the wrong points. Similarly the Church seems at times to ignore or repudiate the new sources of life which scientific knowledge and scientific method have made available. On the other hand she seems to be unaware of the deep divergence between the basic assumptions of modern culture and the central affirmations of the Christian faith. The secular forces of modern life have sapped her own strength so that she is ill-equipped spiritually for recognizing this divergence or for the task of re-expressing her central faith in fresh thought and life. Of course there are many individuals and many groups within the Church of whom these statements are quite untrue. Therein lies the hope for effective Christian education. But we are concerned here with general trends and one condition of the cure of our present ills would seem to be a clearer and more widespread understanding of the nature of the disease.

III

What of the contribution to be made to Christian education by the school? A similar set of difficulties meets us in that sphere. With the growth of national school systems the problem of religion and education has been dealt with differently in different countries. In Britain, for example, education still nominally has a Christian basis. We point to the fact that public opinion has stood unfalteringly behind religious teaching in schools provided by the state, although it is open to any local education authority to omit it, and we congratulate

K

ourselves complacently that the country is Christian at heart in spite of all the evidence to the contrary. Yet what is this "Christian education" of which we boast? Closer inspection may well destroy our complacency. No mere criticism of technical efficiency is implied. Scripture has a recognized place in the curricula of our schools and the standard of teaching is certainly rising. No doubt the position is far from satisfactory, especially in many of our secondary schools. But there is a general awareness of the problem on its technical side and much is being done to improve scripture syllabuses and ensure adequate training for teachers. All that is valuable, but it does not touch the root of the problem.

The more effectively scripture is taught the more clearly it may be expected to reveal the inherent contradiction in the present situation. The school is bound to reflect modern life and the curriculum of the school is deeply influenced by modern culture. But modern life and culture are sub-Christian or un-Christian both on the ethical and religious level. Capitalist society, which sets man against man in the struggle for material well-being, is essentially immoral, while the prophets of a new social order witness to the strength of the secular spirit by their attempt to combine ethical idealism with metaphysical naturalism. A double difficulty thus arises from the presence of Christian teaching within a national system of education. If such teaching is effectively related to social realities it will provide a searching criticism of the social order which may not be welcome in a state school. If it is not so related it will dissolve in a rosy haze of sentiment and emotion, while the recognized standards of the everyday world remain the real guide for conduct. There is also inevitable tension between the scripture lesson with the religious view of life which it implies and the secular presuppositions which underlie the curri-

culum as a whole. Most of the regular school subjects
cultivate the critical inquiring attitude and focus attention on the world of nature and the temporal interests
of man. The attitude of worship and the existence of
non-temporal realities are recognized mainly, if not
exclusively, in school prayers and the scripture lesson.
The two attitudes are not mutually exclusive, but there
is inevitably a latent tension between them. Where it is
unrecognized this tension frequently issues in the collapse
of the weaker element. The religious view of life may
be represented in the curriculum of the state school, as
in Britain, but the intellectual presentation of it is inadequate and the weight of a humanistic culture is over-
whelming. Can we wonder that scientific humanism is
the creed—conscious or unconscious—of a growing proportion of the community?

Our modern school systems reflect the current uncertainty about moral and spiritual values. The schools of
the medieval Church had a clear educational aim. They
recognized man as a spiritual being whose chief end was
"to glorify God and enjoy Him for ever." The words
are those of the Westminster Catechism, but modern
life has moved steadily away from the conception thus
enshrined in the teaching of the Puritan Reformers.
What is the aim of modern education? To that question
there is no clear answer because modern civilization has
no clear sense of direction. The synthesis of all human
knowledge and experience which medieval Christianity
provided has gone and nothing has taken its place. The
collapse of that synthesis was inevitable, nor should we
wish to see a new rigid synthesis take its place. What
we do need is a living faith which is capable of growth
and adjustment with growing knowledge and changing
conditions of life while preserving the permanent truths
of our Christian heritage in their full richness. Such

a guiding philosophy for our common life is essential to its well-being. Such a philosophy would also provide that central purpose which every system of education needs to give it vitality and significance. It is the absence of it which is the real problem of education to-day as well as the deepest weakness in our common life.

IV

Here then is our central difficulty. Religious education is being attempted in a community within which the conditions of such education are not present because the governing values of that community have become largely secular. There is no guiding philosophy which determines modern values, for the secularization of life has been a gradual process and largely unconscious. When conscious paganism rears its head large numbers of men recoil from it. Yet they have no effective alternative. That philosophy is the logical outcome of a process in which they themselves are immersed. Modern man is perplexed by the complexity of his own nature and is uncertain of his destiny. At the heart of that uncertainty lies the question: is man made for time only or for eternity? The crisis of modern education and of modern culture is contained in that question. Christianity has an answer to it, but that answer has become formal and threadbare.

Man was made for a life of fellowship with God in time and in eternity. But men and women must be continually regenerated and sustained by divine grace if they are to enter into that life and continue in it. And that life implies a redeemed community as well as redeemed individuals. We need a deeper, more realistic apprehension of the meaning and significance of these statements. The life and thought of the Church have been deeply affected

by modern humanism, and the Church as a whole has
lost both the realistic pessimism and the profound optimism which belong to the classic Christian conception of
human nature and destiny. At the same time she has
become entangled in the ethical standards of a temporary
social order, and has failed to provide a realistic analysis
of contemporary society from the standpoint of eternal
values.

There are many signs of a new movement of the spirit
in our time. A consciousness of religious need is widely
manifest. The facts of social life are being more realisti-
cally faced, and Christians are finding themselves compelled to seek a more profound religious understanding
of human life. It is out of this fresh stirring of the spirit
that more effective Christian education may be expected
to emerge. The Communist analogy of the "cell" gives
an excellent picture of the way in which fresh insight
spreads. The whole machinery of Christian education
through Church or school must be maintained and
improved, but the solution of the present crisis in Christian education lies with those groups of men and women
who are sensitive to the intellectual and social issues of
our time and, impelled by them, are seeking a more
profound Christian insight. Nor will the conditions of
effective religious education be present within the Church
as a whole until the answer to that question of man's
nature and destiny comes again with new conviction out
of a deep, disturbing experience of the Living God.

CHRISTIAN EDUCATION IN THE WORLD OF THE PRESENT DAY: ITS NATURE AND ITS MISSION

by

PH. KOHNSTAMM

CHRISTIAN EDUCATION IN THE WORLD OF THE PRESENT DAY: ITS NATURE AND ITS MISSION

I. SOME BASIC CONSIDERATIONS

1. *Definition of our task*

The preceding papers, especially those of Clarke and Smith, have made us acquainted with the twofold crisis in which current education finds itself involved. On the one hand, they showed us the contrast between the way in which education is understood by the totalitarian and by the liberal-democratic state. Whereas in the former the whole emphasis is laid on educating the members of a community to take their place in that community, education in democratic countries—although not always in theory, yet actually in practice—insisted rather too strongly on the central importance of the education of the individual. On the other hand we saw that the type of education which has been traditional in the Church is in a very critical position, as the result of secularist attacks which have had an extensive influence.

It is for other writers in this series of volumes to investigate whether these two apparently quite different conflicts are at bottom interconnected, and especially to try to find out whether the whole phenomenon of the emergence of the totalitarian state (in the sense which is here spoken of) is not a consequence of this process of secularization. Hence in this paper I will not discuss this question any further, but will simply express my conviction that secularization (i.e., the process by which man's awareness of himself as a creature of God is destroyed) must always and everywhere lead to an exaggeration of the power of the state.

Further, within the limits of this volume, it is not possible to open up the whole question of Christian education. Our problem is not "the Church and Education," but the relation between Church, community, and state in the sphere of education. But those who take part in the oecumenical discussion on this theme will be continually at cross purposes unless they begin by coming to some agreement as to what is meant by "education" within the sphere of the Church, and, as a consequence of that, what rights are of necessity to be conceded to the state in educational matters. And such an explanation of the idea with which we are dealing is the more necessary because in German-speaking countries, and in German pedagogical literature, the word "Erziehung," which seems to be equivalent to "education," has a humanistic significance, which makes it extremely difficult to understand why in other languages what seems to be equivalent has indeed another meaning.

So this makes it necessary to examine at least shortly what is meant by Christian education.

2. *Education and Evangelization*

Those for whom the Bible contains the supreme standards know that each individual human being, and therefore each child, stands in a direct relation to God, and that no one has any right to interfere with his neighbour in this relation of dependence on God. Living as we do in a civilization which has been profoundly influenced by Christianity, we find that these ideas have also influenced secular education. The first effect of their influence has been that this Christian reverence for the conscience of others has produced a state of mind in which we shrink from trying to control and determine the lives of others. This negative pedagogy is to be found in Rousseau, Tolstoy, and Ellen Key; in the pedagogy of humanism and socialism on the Continent, it gives rise to the conviction that "letting a child mature and grow up" should take the place of authority. But this pedagogy without authority becomes a danger to state and to society. Hence further change in secularized education, which again can be seen very clearly in Rousseau; the education which he begins in "freedom" finally enslaves the pupil, since it attempts to make the pupil's will wholly subject to that of the educator. Speaking generally, it can be said that throughout the area of secularization what happens is that an earthly authority gives itself out to be divine, or at any rate allows itself to be given out as such, on the ground that only in that way can authority be maintained. Now what Christian education means can be best presented by way of contrast to this aberration. Christian education is the action of one who is aware that he can never become the ultimate source of authority for another, but that he *can* make him feel that both of them alike stand before the only real authority, that is, the authority of God. To that extent, education has the same aim as evangelization, and especially as missionary work, since in the latter term the relation of the more to the less advanced is implicit from the outset. In comparison with this agreement on essentials, the differences are of a secondary nature, and arise from the fact that in the case of education we are dealing with differences in maturity which are conditioned primarily by the succession of generations, and, in the case of missionary work, with differences arising from another source. So we do not doubt that in education also we can and should hold fast to the words of Paul, in which he speaks of our being labourers together with God. He gives the increase, while we have to plant and water; but youth remains God's husbandry and ought to be God's building.[1]

[1] 1 Cor. iii. 6-9.

A further result of this is that we are freed from the convulsive efforts to which a secularized education almost of necessity leads when it takes its task in dead earnest. A Christian is resigned to the fact that he cannot himself do what is ultimately and pre-eminently required; he may, and indeed he must, leave that to God. Faced with the task of preparing the next generation to meet the demands of state and community, Christian education goes soberly to work, because the reality in which it is rooted is that of a fallen world. A certain compulsion in education is, therefore, indispensable, but we must neither enhance it in romantic fashion nor use religion to cast a glamour over it, but it must arise naturally out of the necessities embodied in social, economic, and cultural facts.

This sobriety on the part of Christian education is in marked contrast to the pedagogy of humanism and idealism, inasmuch as it has courage to exact discipline, and in particular courage to *punish*. For no education which works at the level of human autonomy does or can produce this kind of courage, for the reason that it does not know the meaning of forgiveness and grace. But, in contrast to the "will-to-education" of the totalitarian state, this sobriety of Christian education is to be seen in the way it distinguishes questions of discipline from questions of conscience, while the totalitarian state, which is in essence the repudiation of all limits, cannot recognize any limit at this point. Thus Christian education is freed from the fear that, either, on the one hand, freedom may be lost, or, on the other hand, genuine freedom may have disastrous effects, because it only preserves this freedom in all its range, where what is at stake is really a question of conscience. For it knows—and in this faith it acts—that the whole realm of culture in all its variety— and all human tensions are resolved into a harmony in

Jesus Christ, and this makes it proof against the temptation to bring about a harmony artificially through the application of compulsion.

3. *Jesus Christ as the centre of Christian education*

These last remarks have already indicated what, or rather Who, is the centre of all Christian education. In the centre of all the considerations which follow, we set the confession which the Church makes in every land and every age: Kyrios Christos, Jesus Christ is our Lord.

Of course it is not our intention to enter into the significance of this confession in its whole depth and breadth. We must confine ourselves here to a few brief remarks which are of particular importance for education. What must be emphasized in the first place, is that this confession must not remain a truth which we passively accept, while our feelings and our conduct remain unaltered. On the contrary, it ought to be a profoundly personal relation which gives a new character to the whole of our life. "Jesus Christ my Lord!"—that is not only an insight or a truth at which I arrive, it is, at the same time, an oath of fidelity and an expectation. We yield ourselves to Him because without Him we cannot live, because we know ourselves sustained by Him in all life's troubles and trials, especially in those for which our own sinful hearts are to blame. We want to be Christians because we know that only in Christ is the world's salvation.

This also means that we have attained the knowledge that only through Him is real human fellowship possible. To be sure, there does exist an intercourse between men on a purely "natural" basis, and just this association at the level of impulse or instinct shows itself at work with appalling obviousness in the mass-movements of our time. But it is clear that in them common aggression creates the feeling of community, and the community, on the other hand, favours hatred against those who do not belong to it. Love, which is quite different from this instinctive association—in the Greek, *Agape* and not *Eros*—is always derived from Christ, whether it is aware or not that its origin is in Him. And the more aware it is of this origin, the stronger and nobler the forms will be into which it develops. This is shown in every type of human fellowship; for whether we are concerned with friendship, or the love of husband and wife, love between parents and children, love of one's people or of an individual belonging to one's people, or of humanity, all these are constantly being imperilled by our self-assertion and desire for mastery, our weakness, cowardice, and blindness.

But, in Jesus Christ, we find the way to God as the source of all love, goodness, wisdom, and power. He has taught us what prayer is, and in His name we venture to pray, strange and full of contradiction though such a venture must be in all eyes, which He has not opened. For how is "natural reason" to understand that an omnipotent God concerns Himself with the words of small, frail creatures, that a holy God has compassion on sinners, yes, seeks them in a world that would be lost without Him? Only as we yield ourselves to Christ's call does such a confidence become reality for us, only as we do so does life win a firm basis, and our thought and action gain certainty and direction.

Now Christian education is simply the attempt to be of service to a young person so that he may find this way of "trustful obedience" (I borrow this translation of *pistis* from Delekat's version of *Romans*). For the child in his natural state is not familiar with it. When, in Matthew xviii. 3, children are pointed to as examples for adults, we have no right to interpret what is said as though that were the case; rather must we read the passage in connection with Matthew xix. 14, where it is said that we are not to forbid children to come to Christ, which means that when they get to know Him they feel themselves attracted to Him. In the Christian family, and in every other form of society which is based on Christ, modes of living are developed which help to demolish the hindrances which are caused by the purely "natural" life.

But we hinder the children's approach to the Master quite as much by what we leave undone as by what we do. There is such a thing as giving either too much or too little help, and also of giving the wrong kind of help. In the next section we shall deal with these points in more detail; here we must emphasize that in Christian education we are concerned with the *whole* life of the young person. The whole life—this means consciousness and being, thought and action. Education is more than instruction, and works at a deeper level than the appropriation of knowledge which can remain isolated from disposition and action. And education is also more than habit-formation, the imprint of forms of conduct which appear to be permanent, but really are only impressed from the outside. Education cannot dispense with instruction nor with habit-formation as auxiliaries, but it is itself more than these. It is a way of living together which enables the older and the younger generation to share a common life of such a character that, in the course of it, something of the meaning and worth of the world and of human life dawns on the younger through the words and deeds of the older. But this must become the younger generation's own possession; and that can happen only when the educator is aware that he is there to *serve*, but not to *rule*, to be of assistance to youth, but not to take the work and the responsibility from their hands.

Especially, at this point, must we bear in mind the

following words of Oldham: "In one of the most decisive and revolutionary of His recorded sayings, Jesus drew the sharpest distinction between the values of His own Kingdom and those prevailing in the world. 'Ye know,' He said, 'that the rulers of the Gentiles lord it over them, and their great ones exercise authority over them. Not so shall it be among you.' He illuminated in a flash the problem of power, which is central in the relation of men with one another, and which in spite of its importance has received less attention from Christian thought than it deserves."

For from this it follows immediately that Christian education aims at responsible living: i.e., the life of a man who stands in direct intercourse with God, knows himself to be addressed by Him, answers Him, and listens to what He has to say. To that extent, it is also an independent way of living: i.e., it is not directly dependent upon other persons. Of course this does not by any means imply a life in isolation, for God, as He has revealed Himself in Jesus Christ, constantly refers us to our neighbour, and only through this reference does a man find the right attitude to his neighbour.

A young person, however, finds this way in a community and not in isolation. Just as his intellect is not developed but crippled if he grows up outside the living community constituted by those who speak his mother tongue, so he needs a full and deep common life in order to grow up in faith, i.e., in trustful obedience to the Father of Jesus Christ. Without the example of others and intercourse with them, he will not even know what these words mean.

II. DEFECTS OF TRADITIONAL EDUCATION

The recognition that human fellowship has such a far-reaching influence also means, however, that it raises the fateful question: Has the fellowship of Christ, the Church, hitherto sufficiently expressed her own insights and principles in education? Does the twofold crisis with which we are concerned possibly mean that Christianity has not done enough planting, and has not adequately watered the young plant?

"Every man shall receive his own reward according to his own labour."[1] Is perhaps this twofold crisis in which the world is now involved the reward of an educational activity which took its work too lightly? In this section we will deal with five of the main reasons which seem to justify an affirmative answer to this question: in so doing, however, we do not assert that there are not other important causes, either inside or outside the sphere of education.

4. *Intellectualism*

The first and perhaps the most dangerous error of traditional education is its intellectualism. In fact, it seems as though the traditional view, at any rate on the Continent of Europe, regards education as an affair of the head rather than of the heart, and pays more attention to the formulation of correct theological formulae than to a life of trustful obedience. The penalty for this has been heavy. I give one example, which could easily be multiplied. Günther Dehn summarizes as follows an enquiry he conducted covering several thousand young people in Berlin:

"In no instance can we discover any trace of a personal relation to the person of Jesus in any boy or girl. In general, Jesus is seldom mentioned. When He is, He is either regarded quite in the traditional way, as the miracle-working Son of God (His *words* do not play any

---

[1] 1 Cor. iii. 8.

part), or as the first Socialist. No one seems to know what is meant by faith, nor what is meant by communion with God or a life lived in His sight . . . . Of course, the fact that very often orthodox ecclesiastical dogmas were reproduced in the essays makes no difference to this picture."

Here we see the root of the disaster which threatens Christian education as a whole and Christian religious instruction in particular. Far be it from me to deny the importance of theological formulation, as though one should claim that Christian living, and therefore Christian education, are possible without knowledge and so without instruction. But the more I have studied not only children and young people, but adults as well, the clearer has it become to me that doctrine can only really mould life when it is itself the expression of an experience that is anchored deeper in our personality than any purely intellectual knowledge or understanding. Here there is a certain movement, a dialectic between consciousness and the deeper emotional and volitional strata of human nature, to which our traditional "Christian instruction" seldom does justice.

To me it seems quite clear that this over-estimation of the intellectual factor in education is linked with the fact that the Churches of the Continent are too exclusively in the hands of students of theology. Laymen, and especially women, would give a different emphasis from that which is common to the traditional type of education; hitherto they have had far too little responsibility for such development. This has made faith too much of an abstraction, while its connection with daily life and its activities has fallen into the background. And this inclination to abstraction which is inherent in all theology, just because it is not living faith itself, but a *scientific exposition* of that faith, is still further strengthened by the fact that even to-day the prevailing theology is of scholastic, i.e., Aristotelian origin. But the "unmoved Prime Mover" of Aristotle is an abstraction which has only a slight connection with the Father of Jesus Christ as He is revealed in the Old and the New Testament. How vast a difference there is between the two we discover, to our amazement, when we compare one of the current catechisms, or a text-book of religious instruction, alongside of *Green Pastures*, the negro play which has created such a sensation, and in which we are shown how the Bible is taught to negro children, and then reflect that the Bible itself is incomparably nearer to this primitive and concrete presentation than to the abstractions of theology. Let no one object that it is precisely the intellectuals who are affected primarily by the apostasy of our day, and the mass of the people only as influenced by them. For in the deepest needs of his life the intellectual of our own day is a thoroughly primitive person who has lost his way in life, and cannot find it again with the aid of his positivistic science. He is a ship without compass or rudder. In this, I am completely in agreement with J. W. D. Smith when he says:

"A guiding philosophy for our common life is essential to its well-being. Such a philosophy would also provide that central purpose which every system of education needs to give it vitality and significance. It is the absence of it which is the real problem of education to-day as well as the deepest weakness in our common life."

I am firmly convinced that we not only need such a philosophy, but that it is already to be seen in outline among us. Its working out and further development will, of course, not be the affair of the individual, but rather the task of earnest collaboration within the Church.

But this work must not be exclusively, nor even primarily, directed towards man as "knowing," if, that is, we take the word "knowledge" in the sense of Greek philosophy and not in the Biblical one. For in the latter sense, the "knowledge of God" is not so much a concept of God as a life with Him.

This, however, brings us to our second point.

5. *The under-estimation of activity*

It is one of the most perilous consequences of the view of education with which we have just dealt that man's co-operation in God's plan of salvation is under-estimated. In fact, the idea of an Almighty God who yet needs weak and sinful men as His fellow-workers is a thought which is "foolishness" to Greeks of every land and every age. All the same, it is an essential element in the Gospel. And it is a Gospel with a peculiar appeal for children and young people. Children and young people do not understand the view that there can be such a thing as trustful obedience which does not bear fruit in daily life. And if they were theologically trained, they could appeal for confirmation to the greatest theologians of the *Una Sancta*, not only to Roman Catholic doctrine, but even to the Heidelberg Catechism, though in this case from a different angle.

Merely as a matter of theory, therefore, to insist that Christian life—and so Christian education as well—must take cognizance of action, will meet with little or no opposition. It is all the more remarkable, therefore, that in practice the kind of education which has remained on the traditional basis scarcely ever provides the impulse to activity with an opportunity to express itself. Certainly, in the devotional part of a service, the child has been accorded sometimes a place which makes him more than a listener. This has been done on the Roman Catholic side by Maria Montessori, and on the Protestant side by some new ventures in Sunday school method, which deserve recognition, such as the movement emanating from Westhill. But such procedure is exceptional and does not cover what is in my mind essential. For a religious service can very easily be divorced from the rest of life as an aesthetic experience which remains apart from the formation of the whole man. This danger is particularly to be feared in the case of the child, because his psychical life is still so far from having achieved unity. The child and the young person equally fail to see the connection between such an experience and simple daily life; it is in danger of becoming an experience for Sunday, which has no point of contact with daily life.

But it is at this very point that the child's need lies: he needs to learn to see the things of daily life in the light of obedience to God's claim on him. If anyone objects that this means over-emphasizing the law at the expense of grace, he has not yet understood why Paul (in Gal. iii. 24) calls the law a schoolmaster to lead us to Christ. It is by following the law that we become confirmed in obedience; and the danger that one may learn to pride oneself on one's obedience can easily be guarded against in the Christian family-circle, where every day our mistakes come to light so clearly and in such detail. At least, that is the case if only the educators have a clear knowledge of themselves, and are not too arrogant, nor feel themselves too much on a pedestal, to go so far as to join with the child in a common confession in the presence of God.

This is obviously not the place to discuss the many problems which the Oxford Groups raise for us. But I would like to emphasize this one point, that, to my mind, we have here undoubtedly one of the reasons why in many countries the Oxford Groups are growing into what is perhaps the one Christian mass-movement of our day, and why they exercise so strong an attraction for young people on the threshold of manhood and woman-hood.

Closely connected with this need to bring not only our thought and speech, but also, and especially, our action, into the service of God, is the need for an understanding of the Gospel which does not confine it to the next world. That this earth is only a "vale of tears" and "lies wholly in the wicked one" is an incomprehensible idea for young people even in a time so exceptionally gloomy and threatening as the present. I am convinced that in this they are more in accordance with the Bible than those who follow that pietistic view, which is solely interested in the next world, a view which is still wide-spread even in our present-day education, at least outside the Anglo-Saxon countries.

I shall have to come back to this point in another connection. Here I will only remark that there is a close relation between it and the controversy often spoken of as that between the Continental and the Anglo-Saxon types of presentation of the Gospel. It is common knowledge that the former type often rejects somewhat disdainfully the world-acceptance of the latter and the optimism of its social Gospel. And, for my own part, I must admit that I too often find the expressions against which this criticism is directed inadequate and over-simplified, when considered as theological statements. I do not see how a presentation of the Gospel can do itself justice without an eschatological and other-worldly element. But as a student of educational problems, I cannot shut my eyes to the fact that it is precisely in the Anglo-Saxon countries—though perhaps one should include Scandinavia as well—that secularization has, comparatively speaking, done least to crowd the Church out of its place in public life. Can it, perhaps, be the case that in these countries, though their theology may be

more open to question, the churches have made themselves
more intelligible to laymen with no theological training,
and to young people in particular? I do not raise this
question here with any intention of offering an answer
to it; but it seems to me of the very greatest importance,
and something which deserves and needs our thought
and prayer.

6. *False emphasis on distance*

Closely connected with the danger of under-estimating
Christian action, i.e., action planned and carried out in
obedience to Christ, lies the danger of stressing too much
the feeling of "distance" in education. I mean by this,
asking children and young people to see their whole life
from the standpoint of the Cross. If we follow closely the
quotation from Günther Dehn we shall see the disastrous
consequences of such an attitude. Jesus as the miracle-
working Son of God, whose teaching has no part to play,
and to whom, therefore, one does not stand in any
experiential and personal relation—this is at bottom the
old Docetic heresy, but even now it seems hard to eradicate
it from preaching, pastoral work, and education.

Certainly it is easier to use correct expressions about
Christ than so to yield oneself to Him that He takes shape
in us, and His power so shines through our weakness
that it lays hold on all who come in contact with us.
And yet it is precisely that which is of more effect in
education than anything else. This being the case, we
must not be ashamed even of our weakness. As we have
already emphasized, the traditional Christian education
still builds too much on the sand of human authority,
instead of on the rock of God's authority. To be sure,
even in Christian education, there is a position of authority
for parents and educators, or rather it is precisely here
that there is such a position; yet woe to us if we forget

that this authority can only be a temporary substitute
for another! Herein, I think, lies a serious failing on the
part of traditional education, in Christian circles as
elsewhere; I mean that it is not sufficiently aware of the
danger we all constantly run of wanting to rule instead
of to serve. The pride, i.e., the disobedience of the adult,
is almost always partly responsible for the disobedience
of his pupils. Out of the huge mass of literature on the
subject of education, I know few books which take this
fact sufficiently into account. And it is at a time like the
present, with its apparent emphasis on authority (though
unfortunately only too often it is really the worship of
violence), that we are doubly tempted to forget that
Christian education at any rate must follow a different
line of action. I am well aware that I should never have
perceived the full bearing of this truth had it not been
for the great assistance which the new psychology renders.
I shall return to this under section 9.

Here I wish to point out yet another aspect of this
wrong feeling of "distance." It is one of the splendid
"foolishnesses" of the Bible that God, the Almighty
Creator of heaven and earth, is concerned for the individual and what befalls him. But actually, in circles
which we usually speak of as definitely Christian, people
frequently live as though it were only the "great and
important" decisions of their life which involve them in
a relation to God. The worship of God is something which
belongs to Sunday, and possibly to certain moments in
daily life which are of a serious and important character.
But that each of our acts down to the minutest detail—
the way in which we say "Good morning!" or give an
order, or look for the newspaper that is mislaid—is an
essential expression of our inner self and ought to be
brought under God's discipline, is frequently denied.
We must not bring such "trifles" into connection with

God! But for children there are no trifles in this sense. What seems to us unimportant may be bitter earnest to them, and their vision is often clearer than ours. Christian education has never yet reckoned deeply enough with Matt. xviii. 6 and its serious implications. And in part at least, it is what we have sown in such "trifles," and in habits that were left to take their course, that is being reaped now in the general secularization and in a world full of resentment and aggression.

7. *The rôle of fear*

"Be not afraid; for behold I bring you good tidings of great joy which shall be to all people!" That is the first public proclamation of Jesus Christ in the world.

Has Christian education always gone to work in this way? How does it go to work nowadays? An answer to the first question may be dispensed with. So far as the second is concerned, we can say that the situation is better than it was a hundred years ago.

> There is a dreadful hell
> And everlasting pains;
> There sinners must with devils dwell
> In darkness, fire, and chains.

In her valuable book on *Child Psychology and Religious Education* (S.C.M., London, 1928), Dorothy Wilson quotes this verse from a collection of the year 1852 as specially written for children. No one will be found to defend it to-day. But anyone who gets his information from the childhood recollections of our adult contemporaries, or possesses the confidence of children and young people, knows that a great deal of this kind of thing is still a reality, albeit in a less gross form. Of course, there are considerable differences on this point in different countries and within a single country. In particular, British friends have told me that my description does not apply to British or American education to-day, and I will gladly accept that, although it does not seem quite to agree with Dorothy Wilson's experiences. And in any case, on the Continent there are still large groups—as, for example, was shown in the discussions at the third Dassel Conference in 1936 of Christian workers among boys and girls of secondary schools—which need to be warned against this mistake. Of course, in so doing, we must be on our guard against the opposite temptation to a too "friendly" attitude in the course of education. We must not think of touching up the stern features in the portrait of our Lord, the Judge of the World, so as to produce a "liberal portrait of Jesus." To adults, and perhaps also to young people, there were words of unsurpassable severity and warning spoken by the Lord. But nowhere in the Gospels—I think one can say, nowhere in the Bible—are children addressed in that way. Thanks to modern child study, the significance of this fact is much clearer to us than it used to be; but traditional Christian education has not yet appropriated its consequences.

Fear is a frightful poison which does its work in secret; it grows and grows unnoticed and destroys all courage and all trust. Only God who knows the innermost recesses of the heart, knows the course it runs and can control it. And yet perhaps we men have it in our power to thwart His will, when we impress our little-faith and our despair on our children and children's children to the third and fourth generation.

And yet only too often so-called "Christian education" does not hesitate to take this road; indeed, it often regards this as the goal at which it should aim. I illustrate by the following, for which I can vouch.

A mentally defective lad of nine came home from the special school he was attending. Still full of what he had heard there of the goodness and love of Jesus, he gave vent to his feelings in the exclamation "God loves us all." The incensed father struck the table with his fist and shouted: "What confounded nonsense! better tell you that you are dead in sin and damnation." The lad stood a moment like one nonplussed and then he thrust out his tongue and ran from the room, shouting impudently, "You know nothing about it, for Jesus likes us all the same." Of course, I am fully aware that this is an extreme case, but it is just by extreme cases that we can bring to our notice what we overlook in moderate ones.

Now my assertion, nay, rather my accusation, is that traditional Christian education acts only too often on this principle, though not to the same extent. It demands that dogmatic judgments should be reached at an age when one is not psychologically mature enough to understand. It abandons the evangelical way—and, to my knowledge, this happens as often in so-called evangelical Christianity as in other parts of the *Una Sancta*—thinking that a man must be thrown into despair for his sins before the Gospel of God's love can be preached to him. But that is to reverse the proper order. The Gospel teaches us that only the assurance of the divine love and grace by which our life is sustained awakens the sense of sin, for apart from this we should not be able to endure it.

> Life is not the highest of things good,
> But the greatest of evils is *guilt*.

So speaks Schiller. But he shows by that that he is a humanist and not a Christian; for if he had been, he would have known that no feeling of guilt is comparable with that sense of utter vileness which the Christian calls awareness of *sin*. This sorest of all human experiences is his only who "comes to himself"[1] as he recalls the seeking

[1] St. Luke xv. 17.

love of his Father, and, to be able to do so, he must know that love.

But it is only the mature man who "comes to himself" in this way. The child is capable of feeling guilty; he knows quite early what guilt is, while his parents are still for him "in the place of God." And then is the time for him to learn what forgiveness is; then he should begin to divine, however dimly—a truth which has remained hidden from a psychologist like Freud up to an advanced age—that the name Father in the Bible does not stand for "the conception of a higher Being who punishes inexorably," and does not possess "the hard, cruel features of an imperious Ought,"[1] but that the Father of Jesus Christ is that God of whom it is said in the 103rd Psalm:

> As far as the east is from the west,
> So far hath He removed our transgressions from us.
> Like as a father pitieth his children,
> So the Lord pitieth them that fear Him.

But only he who knows this compassion can fathom what it means to reject it and to cut oneself off from it. "Herein is love, not that we loved God, but that He loved us, and sent His Son to be the propitiation for our sins." But how is "Christian education" to lead to such knowledge if it confronts the child with an accusation of sinfulness while it is still developing and immature, before it knows love?

8. *Special problems of education of girls*

Up to this point, everything which has been said applies to education as a whole, for boys and girls alike. Un-

---

[1] Cf. Freud's theory of the origin of conscience in his *The I and the It*; his language on the subject of religion, as for example in *The Future of an Illusion*, is only intelligible when this is first understood.

fortunately, we male beings have to recognize that, due especially to our pride, there are special dangers for the other sex. To be "only a girl" is a bitter experience, and, what is worse, a source of disobedience and rebellion for which often the educators must bear the blame. In the same way special dangers attend on the preference which is shown to the eldest son and the greater readiness to make sacrifices for the son or the sons than for the daughters. And, of course, it is not only men educators who are responsible for this: it is quite amazing how often in Christian circles, when the discussion turns on the relation between husband and wife, Genesis ii with its apparent sanction for a privileged position on the part of the husband is appealed to, and how seldom people call to mind Genesis i, where clear expression is given to the co-ordination of the sexes. And further, the saying that "in Christ Jesus there is neither male nor female" (Gal. iii. 28) has as yet hardly received general recognition in Christian education, even where it has secured a "theoretical" recognition, which usually means one which carries with it no obligation to action.

In contrast to this, there is the attempt of humanistic and idealistic education, here as elsewhere, to put equality in the place of equivalence, i.e. to act as if no distinctions existed between the sexes, and in particular to attempt to efface these distinctions by educational measures. Here too we are experiencing a decided reaction against this humanism, and that not only in countries with totalitarian tendencies, and here again our sole protection against the dangers of such one-sidedness lies in clear reflection upon the Christian commandment. And this reflection on the position of woman in the Church is of exceptional importance in the case of educational problems, because there is hardly another sphere in which she is so indispensable as here, and where her special *charisma* is so clearly in evidence. The Church, however—at least in deed, if not in word—has only too little understood this truth. I referred above to this circumstance, and in the sequel I shall return to some gratifying exceptions. Here, I will only emphasize what I said in the previous section, that it is the daily study of psychological and pedagogical— or perhaps it would be better to say anthropological —questions which has shown me the full significance of the fact that, even now in "Christian" circles especially, too commonly the view of human nature which prevails is a patriarchal and not a Christian one. That indicates a further aspect of our problem to which we now turn.

III. THE CHURCH'S TASK

9. *A science of education as a requirement of faith*

Almost every point in the preceding chapter shows that the traditional Christian education is lacking in the necessary insight. Certainly the good-will which is so indispensable is often wanting as well; even a Christian educator *remains* a sinful man who has to admit "the good which I would I do not, but the evil which I would not, that I practise." But so far as we know ourselves and our neighbour, we venture to say that probably this condition does not play as great a part in the sphere of education as in the rest of life.

On the other hand, what we do find there, far more often, is a lack of insight into the disastrous consequences of definite types of action. The over-accentuation of man's inability and nothingness already mentioned (in 4) leads often in Christian, and especially in theological, circles to amazing cases of opposition to planned effort of a psychological and pedagogical nature. In this respect, I agree with what President Arlo Ayres Brown has said in the studies preliminary to this book:

"I wonder if, in addition to the secularization of life in the Christian community, another element in the crisis is not that the Christian community lacks confidence in the educational method, and for that reason refuses to take sufficient pains to improve its educational materials and procedures."

I would go even further and assert that no small part of the secularization about us is the outcome of this refusal. Is it not only too easy to understand that a new generation is growing up which knows nothing of trustful obedience, if it has never been able to get to know Jesus Christ, or—and this perhaps is even worse—has merely taken over a correct doctrine about Him, without ever meeting Him Himself? The fact that a very great part of our immediate environment attaches to the terms used in the Gospel a completely different meaning from the one intended, puts this beyond question.[1]

This means that I cannot follow President Brown when he goes on to say: "If so, the Christian needs to learn from the Communists and Fascists how ideals can be made effective in the community."

I am convinced that we can only learn from the study of Communist and Fascist methods—and, for that reason, we ought not to cease studying them—how *not* to go to work. For these methods could not exist—although perhaps their adherents would wish it were otherwise— without continuous incitement and instigation of hate and resentment against our neighbour, in so far as he does not belong to our party, our nation, or our race. Such methods are acts of violence, even if it is only a question of "psychological" application. But Jesus Christ

[1] See on this the excellent remarks of Delekat in the Preface to his translation of *Romans* above cited (Quelle und Meyer, Leipzig, 1928).

does not teach us to use violence on our neighbour, not even with the help of psychological technique. Psychology, like every other science, remains a gift of God only where it has learned to give up ruling and to serve in humility. For it is, of course, a gift of God, and I am in complete agreement with Prof. Smith when he says : "Unfortunately, the Church to-day seems to many to have created an unnecessary conflict in the minds of its members by failing to welcome and assimilate the vast store of new knowledge with which modern science has enriched our lives. She seems hesitant and suspicious in her attitude towards the newer sciences of personality and of social relationships. She does not seem conscious of the profound spiritual significance of modern psychology's contribution toward the cure of souls."

But what are the reasons for this attitude? I see two reasons, externally apparently very different, though possibly they are ultimately derived from the same source. The first is a certain conservatism, a confidence in intuition and tradition as opposed to what is consciously and deliberately planned, and is, therefore, suspected as savouring of a superficial rationalism. Certainly this negative attitude is quite intelligible. Far too often has the attempt been made, in the name of some sort of "science," to impose on Church people as unquestionable truths all sorts of uncritically accepted ideas which happen to be in the air. Too often has some intellectual infirmity covered its nakedness with the prophet's mantle of genuine science. The really scientific attitude of mind presupposes an intellectual mobility, a faculty for thinking things all over again, such as one cannot demand of the vast majority even of Church people. If, therefore, this demand of scientific study of education is made, and especially if it is insisted on in a spirit contrary to that of love, it is only too plain that such a procedure merely provokes opposition. Of course, with all this the Church of all places should never forget that God's revelation does not take the way of ecstasy but of understanding (1 Cor. xiv); that the true Logos is Christ, and Christ the true Logos.

Still worse, of course, is it when these and similar notions belong to the foundation on which a theological system is erected. This view was formerly often the ruling one in pietistic circles. And in the rejection, not only of psychology, but of every attempt to construct any Christian view of science, this attitude seems to have assumed a fresh form in modern theology. This is all the more remarkable, because to the theologian of all people it must be clear that what he is concerned with is not faith itself, but just theology, i.e. a scientific treatment of faith.

It cannot, of course, be the aim of this paper to enter more closely into this weighty problem of what a Christian view of science is, and how it can be attained; that enquiry belongs to other parts of the oecumenical work.

Here, I would only like to dispose of an obvious mis-understanding. My idea of a Christian view of science is not affected by the doubts which Wiesner has raised in his admirable contribution on the problem of social institutions and the Law of Nature against, for example, a "Christian sociology" and that for two reasons. In the first place, because there he is challenging a type of science which wants to exclude the historically con-ditioned and claims to reach results which are valid universally for all periods, countries, and nations. Such a demand, however, is only possible if one's starting-point is a theory of ideas and of knowledge which rests on Platonic and Aristotelian metaphysics or on the Pantheism of the Renaissance, views which rule even present-day thought to a great extent. It is incompatible with a type

M

of thinking, which always is aware of the fulness of creation, and does not explain away the differences as unessential. In the second place, such a "science," as Wiesner rightly points out, derives its norms from reason and not from revelation; i.e. it builds upon a foundation quite other than that which is laid in the Bible. For there can really be no doubt that from the Biblical point of view man does not create norms nor does he find them "in the inner light," but that he knows them by revelation in Christ.

But, provided the term is understood to include these assumptions, not only is there meaning in speaking of a "Christian approach to science," but this Christian approach is the only real and true one. To hold oneself at Christ's service and in this service to investigate the problems of this world does not mean to import human prejudices into facts, but it means that one has won the key which opens the way to a true interpretation of the perceived and the given. It ought to be superfluous to emphasize that in saying this I do not deny the value of what has been added to our knowledge in the last centuries by science, starting from other assumptions Quite the reverse; it seems to me that Christianity should be profoundly ashamed that these gifts have been far richer than the contributions which have been forthcoming within the sphere of the empirical Church. But what has been found thus is and remains a fragment in another and deeper sense than that in which *all* thinking in this aeon must be fragmentary. And even where these fragments seem to fit in easier to a whole than in Christian vision—as in the theories of Enlightenment, of Evolutionism, and Darwinism, in the economic theory of man as *Homo economicus*, and also in certain findings of modern psychology, especially of psycho-analysis—it is always a case of overhasty and therefore shortsighted generalization and abstraction, the untruth of which must come to light sooner or later. For One alone is the Way and the Truth, who remains such everywhere and for all time.

This view has a twofold significance for the problem of Christian education. For Christian education, in the proper sense, is only possible on the basis of the Christian view of human nature. And this view must be renewed and regained in continual scientific work. If we have a task in God's service, it is worth all our attention, especially in intense and systematic thinking. A study of personality, its willing, feeling, and thinking, is needed for all questions of character formation, i.e. the help which adult and more mature persons can give to younger and not fully-developed ones.

But there is yet another connection between science and education. Instruction, of course, does not cover the whole field of education, but it is an important part of it. In the last resort, however, all instruction leads to questions of *Weltanschanung*, which cannot be left unanswered. And the way in which these questions are answered may seriously hinder and injure. This means that genuine Christian instruction—and this applies just as much to Biblical instruction in the stricter sense as to that in any other sphere—demands the utilization of all the results of relevant Christian thinking. Here the very best is no more than good enough. Certainly there are distinctions of degree, conditioned by circumstances of various kinds, in the first place, by the subject one is teaching and the age of the pupils. The more remote from life the subject, the less will be its influence on central decisions. So that instruction in mathematics will be much less affected by them than that in biology, and this again less than that in history and literature. On the other hand, a form of instruction which is so central as Biblical instruction raises far less intricate questions for the teacher's reflection and training when the teaching is done at the level of the child, than in the case of youth.

10. *The education of educators*

Only now have we reached a standpoint which commands such a wide view that we can speak of the Church's task and then of the state's task in education. But, at this point, we shall again fall into ambiguities unless we bear in mind Oldham's warning: "When action of the Church is proposed, it is always necessary to ask by what persons it is intended to be carried out. Lack of clearness on this point means evasion of responsibility. Action by the Church may in practice mean several entirely distinct things. It may mean action imposed or recommended by the authorities of the Church. It may, on the other hand, be intended to refer primarily to action by the clergy. In this case, a further distinction has to be made, i.e. whether what they do is done in their capacity as ministers and office-bearers of the Church or whether they are acting as individuals and private citizens. Or again, the action intended may mean action by the Christian laity, either in the faithful discharge as Christians of the duties of their vocation, or as associating themselves for the achievement of particular social and political ends, the pursuit of which they believe to be demanded by loyalty to the Christian profession. When the laity so act, they act, or ought to act, as members of the Church, though not as its official representatives. All these forms of action are quite different from one another, and failure to distinguish between them and the unreflective use of a general term ' church,' to cover wholly distinct forms of action, has perhaps been one of the principal hindrances in the way of a true and fruitful understanding of the functions of the Church in the social and political spheres."

Following these directions, therefore, I will go on to

speak briefly, without raising any claim to completeness, of the responsibility of the most important categories of members of the Church who are called to take part in education: viz. parents, youth leaders, professional teachers in the various types of schools, and official teachers of the Church.

I mention the parents first, because their responsibility for education appears first in the child's life and is more deeply anchored than any other in the act of baptism. But also because they are and always remain the child's most important and most influential teachers; apart from a few exceptional cases, it is with them that the initiative rests for the child's baptism. And this is still the case even in our age of secularization and the accompanying loosening of family ties.

To be sure, in our secularized world, the opinion often prevails that education is primarily a matter of intellectual education, and, therefore, of the school. Unfortunately, this opinion is to be found even among the members of the Church.

So we must strongly emphasize the truth that all who are responsible for education *derive their authority from the parents only*, or, in particular exceptional cases, as a substitute for parental authority. Since this fact, as is attested again and again by the Bible, is grounded in God's order for human life, the influence of the family for good and evil alike is more powerful than any other human influence. The fact that even in Bolshevist Russia the years of early childhood are entrusted to education within the family secures for this influence the most effective sphere of action. For we know to-day—in opposition to the opinions which used to be widespread— that precisely these years of early childhood are of a significance the consequences of which, so far as we can see, can be demonstrated at almost every stage of life. This powerful influence is at work even where, as in the English public school system, boarding-school education has an importance rarely to be met with on the Continent. Of course, I cannot here enter into all the great questions of family education; as I remarked at the beginning, the problem which faces us in these studies is not that of Church and Education, but that of the relation between Church, community, and state in the realm of education. What has been said here is sufficient to justify the conclusion that the Church—meaning by that primarily the authorities of the Church—must champion the rights of parents to educate their children and resist the encroachments of the state. But she has more to do than that; the Church—meaning by this, now, the laity and clergy, the congregations and their leaders—must take her educational task far more seriously than hitherto. Under the influence of the secularizing process of the eighteenth and nineteenth centuries, even in Church circles, the responsibility for education was in the main relinquished or actually handed over to the school; which in most cases meant the state. In part—and this I think is especially true of the Anglo-Saxon countries—such an attitude was due to the still unchallenged presupposition that "general" culture and the foundations on which it rested were really Christian. So that we can regard it even as a gain when this certainty, accepted too uncritically, breaks down. For then parents and other educators again become aware of their full responsiblity.

Perhaps we see this influence most clearly at work in present-day Germany. The primer for the use of mothers issued by the mothers' section of the German Evangelical Women's Auxiliary lies before me as I write. It offers to millions of German mothers direct guidance as to how they can prepare themselves for what is central in their educational task, now that it has become clear to them that they cannot entrust this task to others, but must themselves take it in hand.

That illustrates the second point which must be mentioned; education, although perhaps its most important part takes place unconsciously and involuntarily, must not be allowed to go unprepared as a whole. Just as it is not the case that faith is *only* life and not doctrine, so education cannot merely draw on intuition, but there must be an education of educators.

To this indirect work for youth through work for the parents, especially for mothers, those circles seem to me particularly called which hitherto have been mainly engaged in the service of direct work for youth. In the first place, because they can speak to parents out of their knowledge of youth; in the second, because in the case of youth-work there is always the danger that it may rather strengthen than remove those tensions between the two generations which almost regularly appear, unless a genuine relation of confidence obtains between the home and those engaged in youth-work; also because in this sphere almost everywhere a great army of fellow-workers (women especially) is to be found in greater numbers than anywhere else. Further, because a claim for freedom in such work on the part of the Church for young people and for parents can be much more firmly established, even where the state shows totalitarian tendencies, than in the case of the school. And, finally, because direct work for youth does to a much greater extent than the school, at least where this is not a boarding-school, affect the *whole* man and not that one side of him which is intellectual. So that it stands close to the spirit of family education and can exercise stronger influences than those of the school. Certainly the school ought not to be any *mere* place of instruction, as it was only too often in the nineteenth century, at least on the Continent and particularly in the Universities and higher-grade schools. Just because the school exists not simply to pass on knowledge and technical skill, the *training of teachers* is of the utmost importance, much more important than the often so hotly-contested question of the school curriculum. The last position, therefore, in the sphere of education which a Church that has been forced into a defensive attitude has to maintain against a state with totalitarian tendencies, is that of collaboration in teacher-training.

But inasmuch as the school, although it must not by any means be a mere place for instruction and training, still finds in this more special sphere its main task, only a positivistic over-estimate of the intellectual and technical elements can regard it as *the* place *kat exochen* in which education is carried on. The problem of *education* extends much further and lies much deeper than that of the *school*. In all states and nations it is essential that this should be grasped; and wherever state and culture represent a power alienated from the Church and prohibiting a direct influence of the community on the school, this truth can provide both consolation and the courage to do what is possible in the way of education.

The influence of the Church's professional teachers on education, and, therefore, their responsibility, are certainly already considerable, as for example in what we continue in many countries to call "catechism" instruction, although as an educational method the use of the catechism is very much out-of-date. But it seems to me quite clear that a great deal more might still be achieved here. This would happen, in the first place, if the office-bearers of the Church were to concentrate much more deliberately than has been done hitherto on being teachers of teachers, i.e. of parents, youth-workers, and school staffs, or should that be necessary, teachers of the teachers of these teachers. For anyone who has an acquaintance with present-day educational science knows that there is a lack of those whose powers have been developed by a thorough training. In the second place, this would be possible if they were far more aware than has been the case hitherto that this teaching-office in our day no longer devolves exclusively on those who have had a theological training. Our whole ecclesiastical organization is still to too great an extent dominated by the presupposition which went unquestioned in the Middle Ages that all intellectual training outside of a small group of physicians and lawyers was theological. Here, again, we touch on the problem of whether a "Christian" type of science is possible, and again I must decline to go further into it. But let me, at any rate, express this conviction: that the Church can only tackle the problem of the education of educators as it should be done when she definitely calls in the assistance not only of *Christian* theologians (for there are theologians who are not Christians and who do not want to be such), but also the Christian representatives of *other* sciences.

11. *The state's legal claim to education and its limits*

We have already recognized in (2) that the state has a claim to education. For we spoke there of the task of preparing the rising generation to meet the demands of the state. In fact, if the state, even the state whose government is not conscious whence its task is derived, has a task assigned to it by God—then the state *must* demand that education is such as to equip the rising generation to serve this task. Under the conditions of our present-day economic and cultural arrangements, this generally means that the state also provides the necessary means to this end, and at least exercises an oversight over the way in which these means are employed. For, in our present economic

system, it is out of the question to entrust the education
of the great masses of the people simply to private
enterprise.

At least the state exercises an oversight; it is not to
be taken for granted that the state will itself organize
educational associations, schools in the first place. As is
shown by the essay of Morris, and also by the memoran-
dum of the Dutch study-group, it is really quite con-
ceivable, although not usual up to the present, that it
should leave to others, such as the Church or parents'
associations, the task of bringing up a generation of good
and able citizens, because the Church and parents stand
so much nearer than it does to what is deepest and most
central in human nature. The state must, therefore,
confine itself to bringing up "capable" citizens, and not
imagine that it has to bring up virtuous characters, for
it cannot reach this goal with the means at its disposal,
whatever may be the cases so far as Christian education
is concerned.

Of course, if the state cannot discharge its task without
capable citizens it is its duty to provide for something
more than the production of intellectual, physical, and
technical qualifications. When in circles which have
wholly or in part come under the sway of secularization—
(whether they still count themselves as belonging to the
Church or not, does not matter in this respect)—an
advancing individualism and intellectualism, or a sentimental humanism, or the self-asserting notion of autonomy
threatens to destroy the basis of all education by destroying all authority, the state has not only the right, but
also the duty, to intervene and itself to take in hand an
education which will be something more than instruction
and technical training. For there is no education which
is not based on authority, and has not the community
in view.

If I am not greatly mistaken, these are some of the motives which make intelligible, though they do not justify, the claims on education advanced by the totalitarian states, at least in Italy and Germany, and presumably in Russia as well. And it would do an injustice to the totalitarian state were we to overlook the fact that in our age of secularization the state is often compelled to establish new bonds and norms, because the traditional Christian ones, on which the whole of European and American civilization rests, are in danger of breaking down. The empirical Church has no right to complain of necessities for which she must bear part of the blame.

But it belongs to the very nature of the totalitarian state that it knows no limits and, therefore, constantly oversteps its limits, invading the rights of other forms of community life even where they have given it no occasion to do so.

To sum up: if the state, either deliberately or in point of fact, claims to be the sole educator, then the Church— and this applies to the Church as a whole, its office-bearers and all its members—can only answer with the most decided No! This problem is incomparably more important than that of school curricula and the establishment of schools. This is why all supporters of a really totalitarian state, from Plato to Fichte, and the present-day advocates of Communist and Fascist Youth Associations, begin at this point.

This means that the controversy will more and more come to a head over this issue. Where the Church is in a minority and the state is one in which the new heathenism prevails, it can acquiesce in any other demand made on it, even to the prohibition of public worship and evangelistic activity. Under certain circumstances, reverence for the powers that be, which indeed do not exist without God's permission, may be carried as far as that. But when the state wants to usurp education—(I think the preceding discussion had made it clear enough that this is something quite different from a demand that certain items of *knowledge* which are indispensable or serviceable to the community should be given to all its members)—the Church can only answer: "We ought to obey God rather than man." It is clear that in a state committed to the new heathenism this *may* lead to martyrdom. Up to the present, unless I am mistaken, even the Russian anti-God movement has not abrogated parental rights as such in education.

But it is outside the scope of this paper, as of the writer's qualifications, to examine what such a state of things would mean.

At this point, the only fitting thing we can do is to pray that God may give to His Church, the *Una Sancta*, strength, wisdom, and readiness, if part of her membership has to seek her help for such a purpose as this.

THE EDUCATIONAL TASK OF THE CHURCH AT THE PRESENT TIME

by

"X"

THE EDUCATIONAL TASK OF THE CHURCH AT THE PRESENT TIME

THIS paper deals with the problem of education from the standpoint of the Church. That is, we do not propose to treat the question scientifically as a problem in pure education, which would entail a consideration of the ideals that should inspire such an education and the precise ways and means to bring it about. We propose rather to consider what are the educational duties imposed on the Church by the situation actually in force in most European countries to-day. At the outset it had better be said that the author is mainly concerned with conditions now prevailing in Germany, but an attempt will nevertheless be made to emphasize and pick out only those aspects which are typical of the culture prevalent throughout Western Europe. For, in order to deal comprehensively with the educational situation, from the standpoint of the whole Christian world, it is necessary to have a profound insight into the inner changes which have taken place during the last two centuries, and are still taking place, in the soul of European man, so that one can see how far they impinge on Christian belief, and how far and in what way they confront the Church with new duties. This may well be thought an impossible undertaking, and that in any case such a reading of the present situation would be dangerously exposed to error, and at best very imperfect. But what else can we do in an oecumenical enquiry such as ours? At any rate it would profit us little if we attempted to formulate a Christian ideal of education universally acceptable to all churches in all countries, or if we made isolated suggestions for the improvement of the Christian training of the younger generation at home and at school. Such an attempt would result in a purely academic and rather useless piece of work, which could only achieve practical value if the state and society, as educational agents, were willing to adopt and make use of our suggestions. For the Church alone has not, in most countries, the power to transform its proposals into practical politics. Totalitarian states constantly struggle to usurp the influence which Christianity, owing to its past, still exerts on education, especially in the schools. In other countries, the actual practical value of Christian education, as now carried on, is doubtful in the extreme. As against this it becomes increasingly clear that the development of Western European culture makes the following question all important. What value have the Christian faith and the Church for the education of mankind? Is their glory not completely outworn, and is not the respect with which it is customary to surround them entirely due to the inertia resulting from an ancient tradition? What is their true significance, and cannot the educational value once ascribed to the Christian faith be much more effectively realized by the help of modern science and the methods of modern pedagogy?

Once this state of affairs is grasped, the Church is immediately faced with the question how far she may claim to be, not only one among many, but *the* truly decisive educational force without which modern man is heading for destruction and the present-day world is doomed to a painful process of disintegration. The fact that many people consider that the power of the Church has long since been outgrown and superseded is partly due to the fact that she herself no longer clearly realizes the source of her "educative" force or the origin of her real power. In order truly to understand wherein this power consists it is essential that the Church should keep clearly in view her actual position in the modern world, and that she should endeavour to understand this situation in the light of the truth of Jesus Christ. It would be of little avail merely to break out into lamentations over the secularization of the modern world. The Church herself is intimately connected by a thousand ties to the world around her. Only by accepting her own share of responsibility for the problems and needs of the present day and by shouldering her part of the suffering can she hope to be of any use. She must keep clearly before her mind the bitter necessities not only which constrain the nations and society at large, but to which every individual, in all his various relationships, is subject. She must openly admit her share of guilt, and must pray God that He will give her unity and strength, so that she may once more become that which she should always be, namely, "the salt of the earth."

I. THE PRESENT CRISIS OF CIVILIZATION AND THE EDUCATIONAL PROBLEMS ARISING FROM IT

When we wish to express in one word the significant character of the present day, we say "we are living through a crisis of civilization." But what is such a crisis? The situation may be considered from varied aspects because it appears in many quarters. Science, or the general intellectual life of the day, is at a crisis. There is an economic crisis. Democracy is at a crisis. Education has reached a crisis, and finally faith is at a crisis.

If we try and think this situation through from the educational standpoint, we do not mean that a crisis has been brought about mainly because of the insolubility of certain educational problems, or that this is its real cause. The crisis can equally well be regarded from the point of view of the general intellectual life of our time,

N

its economics, or even its politics. However, in each case, if we probe sufficiently deeply, we shall find that the question of the ultimate certainties on which our faith is founded will prove to be the goal towards which each avenue of approach leads. The problems that arise in the field of education have been placed in the forefront merely because education happened to be the special subject chosen for Section IV of the Oxford Conference. The main points which spring to mind when the cultural crisis of the present day is considered from the educational aspect are as follows:

1. *What in Essence is Meant by Education?*—The question sounds purely academic, though actually nothing is further from the truth. For such a question does not even arise in times when men live surrounded and protected by the bulwark of a firm faith and settled moral values. Such men educate without giving much thought to the meaning of education. Whenever such a question crops up, it is a sure sign that the community is uncertain of its right to assume a position of educational authority towards the coming generation. Have we the right to inculcate our ways of life and thought as expressed by our character and manner of life? Whenever men feel so uncertain, even if the doubt remains subconscious, of their right to educate, their uncertainty usually first manifests itself by increased educational activity. People take an exceptional interest in education; much is made of the great responsibility of schools and other educational institutions; educational lectures are popular; new educational methods are devised; new training establishments are founded; educational courses for those about to marry or for young parents are instituted, and so on. But very soon it becomes evident that though all this may be helpful in individual cases, on the whole it may mean no more than that we are treating symptoms and

not attacking the evil at its source. The questions: What actually constitutes education? What is the best way to educate? receive so many answers and assume such protean shapes that the condition of the patient and human existence in general become progressively worse. There are too many doctors prescribing too many cures. The further question: Has the community in which we live, such as it is, even the right to educate? is usually not openly stated. But that is the root question. The Church should therefore take warning, and not let herself be led astray when she is told that, in order to keep abreast of the times, she should adopt as many new educational doctrines as possible, together with their corresponding methods. Her task is rather to insist on the root question: Why is your conscience so uneasy face to face with the young generation whom it is your duty to educate? Ambiguity is always the sign of a guilty conscience.

2. *What is the Highest Aim of Education?*—At this point we come up against the problem raised by the current view that all philosophies of life are merely relative, an attitude which is so very characteristic of the present crisis. It is fortunate that the clash of differing conceptions of life does not in every country take the form of a political struggle sometimes even leading to bloodshed. Where this does not happen, these problems do not stir up the same intensity of feeling; and the schools are saved from becoming the sport of politics. But that does not mean that all is well. For public life in which the young man grows up offers him such a host of philosophies, religions, and opinions that he hardly knows which to adopt. None of them has the binding force of a moral law. Even when school and public life are not entirely dominated by politics, he is still exposed to such a multiplicity of views of life that when the heavy hand

of fate or even of guilt descends upon him, youth will, according to temperament, either be driven to desperate courses, or will adopt a shallow sophistication, or else seek the meaning of human existence in mere physical activity.

3. *In Whose Hands Does the Supreme Educational Authority Lie?*—This question does not mean who is responsible for providing either the external machinery by means of financial grants, or the purely intellectual curriculum of the public system of education. That differs in different countries. In some the state shoulders the main burden, in others responsibility rests on free associations of people in the community. These differences certainly produce important differences in organization, but from our point of view they are not of decisive importance, since the question for us is: Who, at the present day, still possesses real educational authority? Without authority true education does not exist because without authority there can be no true freedom. But at the present day where are we to find the authority which exerts a truly compelling effect on a young man's soul? In his home? In some cases, thank God, this is still true, but in many no longer. In his school? Yes—this is still often the case—but for how long? In his professional or trade associations? Mostly not, and certainly not in the sense in which this was true in the Middle Ages. The Church? The state? The demand for an authority which will exert a truly binding effect on the inner being of man, and the search for *genuine* authority, can be found to-day in all layers of society. It is *the* question. What Clarke tells us of the mind of English youth bears this out, and similar examples can easily be drawn from other European countries.

These three considerations by no means exhaust all that could be said about the present crisis of civilization from the educational point of view. But they must suffice for the present. For it is necessary to show their deeper causes as well as their practical results.

II. CAUSE AND EFFECT OF THE UNIVERSAL CULTURAL AND EDUCATIONAL CRISIS

It was said earlier in the paper that the crisis of our present civilization takes many forms, but in its *every aspect*, whether it is considered from the point of view of economics, politics, intellectual life or education, the problem leads us to the ultimate ground and certainty of our belief. In order to develop this thesis in its completeness it would be necessary to survey the whole process of secularization which European civilization has undergone since the sixteenth century. It would be necessary to show how intellectual life, whether in the domain of science, poetry or the plastic arts, gradually deserted the spheres of Christian thought and feeling; how in politics the Christian hope in the Kingdom of God was transformed into an expectation of the coming of a temporal kingdom of God on earth, so much so that the European bourgeoisie conceived the ideal of a perfect state, Socialism dreamt of the ideal of a socialistic state of the future. In the nineteenth century rapid industrialization loosened the ties of village life and of the smaller communities which were so closely bound up with the life of the Church. The larger towns were filled with vast hordes of people with which the Church, with its parochial life adapted to the needs of small parishes, was quite unable to keep pace; the educational influence of Christian custom was gradually frittered away, and one wave of emancipation followed another. We do not propose to give a detailed account of these processes. In any case such a description would only evoke a superficial intellectual assent, and would disregard the inner effect of this universal process of secularization.

Our human existence is rooted in history. That is why the problem of the secularization of life raises the question: who is responsible for the distress which this secularization has brought in its train? It is not much help to explain to human beings that this or that particular effect was produced by such and such a cause. They are not greatly interested, because that will not relieve them of the dire and pressing consequences which this secularization has had on their lives. The ordinary man in the street is usually ignorant of how and why the situation in which he finds himself has been evolved by slow historical processes, nevertheless at certain crises in his life he becomes acutely conscious of the resultant stresses. For instance, he is well aware of the discrepancy which exists between what he hears and reads, in newspaper articles and in the official speeches of ministers, about the universal desire for peace among nations, about the necessity of surmounting the economic crisis, the desirability of maintaining and increasing the standard of life; but his daily life brings him face to face with quite another reality. What he *experiences* is a great absence of peace throughout the world, he finds that the particular corner of the world at his disposal has shrunk, and looks as though it is shrinking still further. Moreover, he has discovered that nothing in this world is entirely secure. Inflation may have destroyed his property, deflation raises the cost of living. How uncertain is money! Why save? In what or in whom can he place his trust? Whom shall he believe? There is no longer any institution which commands universal trust. The Church is considered superfluous; her faith an outworn creed. But do the institutions which have superseded the Church possess his confidence? Man behaves as though he were a "freethinker," but what does this freedom of thought amount to in reality? It simply stands for scepticism and an inner lack of balance—one as desolating as the other, whether it expresses itself as mordant wit or a brutal lack of taste. Social custom no longer exercises any binding control, and this absence of restraint is particularly noticeable in the relations between the sexes. The simplest solution of that particular problem appears to consist in pretending the problem does not exist, although in actual fact it causes much suffering, especially among women. Oft repeated disillusionment produces once again a feeling of antagonism between the sexes, a form of hatred which has peculiarly malignant and life-destroying power. Men despise women; and women despise men. The sanctity of marriage is trodden underfoot, the number of fleeting sexual "affairs" increases; marriage itself is often no more than a legalized temporary union. This inevitably leads to the gravest educational difficulties among the younger generation and produces conflicts and neuroses of all kinds.

All this makes man deeply dissatisfied with his life—a dissatisfaction which expresses itself in endless grievances and complaints. That is why people nowadays are so easily stirred politically; for it must not be supposed that pure political ardour drives such countless millions into the arms of the more violent political parties. Heaven alone knows how much absolutely unpolitical and purely domestic and business irritation finds an outlet in this way. To put it in a nutshell: modern man finds the world a frightening place. It has become too small for him. This does not mean that in itself the world is too small, but it does mean that love has departed from it. For that is precisely the consequence of the secularization of the world, namely, that love is lacking. That is what causes railing, anger, bitterness, hatred, crime, and the insistent demand for the use of force.

III. THE ATTEMPT TO FIND A POLITICAL SOLUTION FOR THE CULTURAL AND EDUCATIONAL CRISIS

Zenkowsky is right when he says that the totalitarian state has not merely been caused by an educational crisis, but that it is also partly the result of political, economic, intellectual, and other conditions. Wherever the totalitarian state is actually in being, the relations of Church and state immediately change. In any discussion of such things care must be taken to avoid the assumption that there exists, so to speak, one normal or ideal standard. The Church possesses certain fundamental articles of belief, which she must uphold in her dealings with the state, and for which she must, if necessary, be prepared to fight. From this conflict there results an actual relation between the two, which may last for a certain length of time, but which will always remain to some degree unstable. It would, therefore, be incorrect to describe the situation between the Church of Jesus Christ and the state as "normal" in a liberal and abnormal in a totalitarian country. The position of the Church in a liberal state is by no means "normal," for even liberalism acts as a check on the gospel of the Christian Church. From the standpoint of liberal politics, Christianity appears merely as *one* conception of life and the world—one among many—and this attitude cannot be reconciled with the saying that in Christ alone can salvation be found, and that the Church is the sole guardian of Christ's truth. It is only necessary to consider how low the credit and influence of the Church fell during the liberal epoch to have striking proof of this. On the other hand, in the case of the totalitarian state with its claim to absolute authority even in matters of faith, the position of the Church, measured by New Testament standards, becomes much more normal. For

once again she is becoming a suffering and a militant
Church. This may be painful for individual Christians,
but it is good for the Church.

At this stage, one should, as a Christian, refrain as
much as possible from all merely human hope and fear;
one should not even try and assess what is normal and
what abnormal, but should confine oneself to obeying
the dictates of one's faith. If the Church is faced by a
totalitarian state she must not regard that state as the
result of human arbitrariness. For the processes involved
go far beyond the possibilities of merely human choice
or the decisions of individual men. The Church must
take a firm stand and react energetically against any
attempt on the part of the totalitarian state to substitute
for God a merely worldly ideal, to erect its own laws
in place of God's laws and to replace the figure of Christ
by a human figure. *But it is equally essential that she should
recognize as a simple matter of fact that the modern state cannot
fulfil its duty if it does not, somehow or other, solve the problem
of how to control and lead the mass of the people.* The way
in which individual states solve this problem may be very
different, and *politically* speaking it may be of the greatest
importance under the aegis of what political ideal this
happens, *but for the Church this is not, and never should be,
the decisive factor.* The Church should never let herself be
harnessed to the wagon of this or that particular brand
of political totalitarianism, but should remember that
the urge towards totalitarianism, which appears to a
greater or lesser extent in all countries where the prole-
tariat has become a major problem, is the ideal in which
people who have long since forgotten all about Christianity and the Christian ideal of society first seek the
solution of their social crisis. It is in that ideal that they
see the only hope of putting a stop to the progressive
disintegration of their social and political life. Their

instinctive reply to the question: What power can supply the necessary unifying influence to restore order once more in the present chaotic condition of human existence? is: "Why, of course, the state." It is only a very small minority who realize that the state, with the political machinery at its disposal, *can at most set up only an outer system of law and order*, but that the *inner* reconstruction of life is bound up with the re-emergence of the power of the Church. Certain experiences through which the totalitarian state (including the people under its rule) are bound to go, are, therefore, necessary in order to increase the number of those who realize the very real value of the Christian faith and the Church. It is possible that a new and stable balance between Church and state can only arise as the result of the conflict forced on the Church by the totalitarian state, a state which is, after all, merely a counterfeit of the Church of Jesus Christ. This experience and this conflict occurs directly the totalitarian state tries to guide and control, not only the outer, but the inner life of man. These experiences are, therefore, part of the new "political education."

A state based on totalitarian principles is by its very nature deeply concerned with education. That is obvious. Every purely intellectual system of thought considers that a planned education is the best way of influencing humanity in favour of a political ideal which alone is considered good and right. This obviously entails a very comprehensive conception of education. The methods of political education include not only schools of every type and grade, but all methods of influencing public opinion. If these methods are rigidly enforced, and the inner gravitation of the mass of the people is still towards totalitarianism, their success is surprising, especially when contrasted with liberal states where signs of disintegration are allowed to appear openly.

As time goes on, however, the following question arises : Is it possible to influence the whole population of a country inclusively in the direction of a single ideal? The idea that this was necessary for the "establishment of the Kingdom of Reason," that in order to achieve this a new kind of education and numerous schools would be required, and that if need be this system would have to be imposed upon the population by force, has already been expressed by Fichte. In his lectures on the doctrine of the state, given in the year 1812, he taught that "humanity, as a refractory entity, ought certainly to be forced, quite ruthlessly, whether it understands it or not, to conform to the sovereignty of law and to the higher truth. This compulsion, however, must be inseparably connected with an institution, in order that this higher truth may become the possession of the whole community. The views of the founder ought, in the course of time, to become the views of all, with no exceptions. Only through the latter will the former become legal." "The compulsive State, therefore, is the school by means of which the Kingdom of Reason, based on truth accepted by all, will be established."

This is no isolated expression of Fichte's ideas. In his second *Address to the German Nation* he says in a similar vein. "The new education must consist essentially in this, that it completely destroys freedom of will in the soul which it undertakes to cultivate, and produces, on the contrary, strict necessity in the decisions of the will, the opposite being impossible. Such a will can henceforth be relied on with confidence and certainty." Without tracing the influence of Fichte in any special way it is quite possible to establish as a fact that, at the latest, about the end of the nineteenth and the beginning of the twentieth century the propagandist activity of the Socialist Parties made an increasing practice of mental terrorism. Here already we see the methods of moral and economic pressure actually at work. Indeed, in Socialist circles one of the most fruitful subjects of discussion has been: How far is it right to go in the application of such methods of terrorism? Thus it would seem as though idealism were fated to develop into terrorism in course of time. Terrorism is a blend of persuasive propaganda and open or concealed threats. If, however, idealism is compelled to resort to such measures in order to be able to assert and maintain its own existence, the question then arises whether both are not inwardly and emotionally opposed to one another? Finally this leads to a purely technical problem: To what extent is it *technically* possible to supervise permanently the outlook of a nation composed of millions of human beings? The perception that this is not possible, and thus, that it is impossible to "annihilate" the free will of man, is obscured at the present time, because the technical aids which the contemporary state has at its disposal make it possible for its organs to have a kind of omnipresence which is feared far more than the divine omnipresence. But the use of these methods almost always produces in those who are subjected to them the fundamental destruction of their belief in the correctness and the inner right of the ideal which is being forced upon them. Thus the ideal which is enforced by the totalitarian state is confronted by an inner barrier beyond which it cannot penetrate.

Further, a philosophy of life which aims at producing certain political results is unable to give an answer to many important questions of life. Man is not *only* a political unit, but each individual has his own fate to bear, his own joys and sorrows, fears and anxieties. What use will a political system of philosophy be to him when death knocks at his door, when he is beset with professional worries or difficulties in his married life, or when his children take the wrong turning?

Church and state are bound to come into conflict, for whenever the concept of a totalitarian state is pushed to its logical conclusion, the attempt is made to replace Christianity by a new religion. This leads to a direct attack on the Christian faith and the Church. It must be freely admitted that in its present condition the Church, in many of its aspects, is simply asking for such criticism; and should, therefore, see in it the scourge of God punishing her for her own misdoings. If, however, she recognizes in the assault made on her by the world a call to repentance, and if she obeys the call, such attacks cannot in the long run do her much harm; though, on the other hand, they may do serious harm to those whom they provoke to merely thoughtless and superficial counter-criticism, seeing only the mote in their brother's eye and forgetting the beam that is in their own. Every conflict in which the weapons of moral slander are used becomes a desperate and hopeless issue, wherein much is destroyed but little built up. To give mankind a new faith, instead of the poisonous fruit of malicious criticism, would mean to realize the kingdom of God on earth by means of political organization and political power—an attempt reserved for the followers of anti-Christ.

A struggle between the totalitarian state and the Church, if conducted by such means, must result in a loss of authority for the state. That is the worst of it; state prisons are not in themselves disgraceful; they only become so because of the sort of people who have to be imprisoned in them and because of the real crimes they have committed. It is a dangerous thing to use them as establishments for political education. For brute force, even when it threatens death, is in the long run the most powerless thing there is.

If, therefore, the attempt of the totalitarian state to solve by educational means the problem of the universal

crisis of civilization is doomed to failure, what then? As
soon as this question is given serious consideration, the
stage is at last reached when it becomes possible really
to grasp the inner and fundamental meaning of the
present crisis, and to recognize that it is in essence a crisis
of faith. For the root of the matter is as follows: The
process of secularization which our present civilization
has undergone during the past several hundred years
attempted to substitute for the transcendent God, who
revealed Himself in Christ, a this-worldly power (namely,
the Spirit of the Universe); and it sought to find the
unity of God and man, not in the person of Jesus Christ,
but in the nature of man himself (i.e. the idea of
Humanity); it hoped for the realization of the kingdom
of God on earth through the ideal future state or the
perfection of human society (secularized eschatologies).
The ideologies current at the time of European liberalism
and humanism represent point by point the transference
of the teaching and the belief of the Church into the
realm of temporal power. And that is true not only of
these political views, but also of the philosophical con-
cepts underlying the totalitarian state. The difference
between liberal and totalitarian ways of thought consists
mainly in the fact that an adherent of the former type
of liberal humanism really believed that his ideas corresponded to the true meaning of life as shown in history;
and that these ideas would, therefore, come to pass *of
themselves* if only mankind could once properly grasp them.
*But modern man who thinks on totalitarian lines has lost any such
belief.* Karl Marx still had such a faith; Lenin no longer
possessed it. As a consequence, an effort is made to substitute a much more concrete ideal for the far-off ideals
of liberal humanism, tainted as these are by Christian
thought; and secondly, since men no longer believe that
the truth of these ideals will of necessity bring about

their realization, an attempt is made to bring this more limited ideal into existence by the use of force. Totalitarian thought conceals the secret doubt that the course of history possesses in reality no inner meaning which man may recognize, other than that imposed on it by his own will. It is this that creates the Superman—that is, a man who proposes to achieve everything by his own strength, which both Christians and humanists have always felt implied convulsive effort.

But it is at this very point that Christians should beware of merely destructive criticism. They should rather recognize that this phenomenon has a certain inevitability about it. A world dominated by humanistic and liberal views reveals its essential nature as loveless, cold, narrow, violent, and brutal. And the world will retain this character until mankind realizes once more the meaning of the verse in the Gospel of St. John xvi. 33. "In the world ye shall have tribulation; but be of good cheer, I have overcome the world." They must learn that God stands in another category than all the values of this world, and must acknowledge His personal revelation in Jesus Christ. They must find their peace in belief in Him—a peace which is not of this world. They must come to know the fellowship of love which can only be realized where the spirit of Christ reigns. All of which leads to the fact that though, as far as modern man is concerned, the Church of Jesus Christ seemed to have disappeared from the realm of everyday life, they must once more experience it as a living reality penetrating from the life beyond into this life. Mankind is suffering from the narrowness of this world and must learn that in Christ God calls them to be citizens of a heavenly world. This necessitates, in the first place, the admission of sin, under whose domination they and the whole world stand; and it will come to pass through belief in their forgiveness and through the experience of the living power of love which springs from the recognition and admission of sin and from faith in Jesus Christ. In so far as small, living Christian communities, possessing this certitude and filled with the hope of a supernatural salvation, come to exist among the disinherited peoples of to-day, will men be freed from all compulsion and learn once more to bear their fate patiently one with another. This is the first step towards a solution of the crisis of civilization.

The Christian, therefore, on the basis of his faith can only understand the meaning of the present crisis in one way, namely, that it is the will of God that once again, in this present unchristian and secularized world, the living Church should arise. That is the meaning of all the suffering imposed on modern man. The reason why such an idea appears so impossible of belief to so many is because they cannot imagine that precisely the Church could ever be of such importance. It is nevertheless necessary to emphasize the fact that the destiny of the Church is the pivot on which the fate of our entire civilization turns. This could be shown in many ways, in the importance of the Church for science, for intellectual life, the legal system, the theory and practice of medicine, and for political and economic reconstruction. Here we will only discuss the question: In what way is the modern problem of education a religious problem?

IV. THE PROBLEM OF FREEDOM

The problem of freedom is the root problem of all education. Clarke is quite right about this. But what is freedom? Obviously this is the point at which Christians of different nationalities understand each other least, because the political conditions under which they live differ too widely. In democratically governed countries,

men will always be inclined to understand by freedom
the recognition of the so-called fundamental rights of a
free personality, and such a conception will obviously
be most firmly and durably ingrained in those countries
where these rights have never been codified, but where
they belong to the self-evident assumptions of social life.
Looked at from such a standpoint, the educational problem will assume the shape that Clarke has given it,
namely, How can the younger generation be educated
so as to retain the ideal of a free personality, while
providing scope for its realization, and at the same time
inculcating discipline, civic responsibility, and public
spirit? I do not wish to criticize this method of stating
the problem. Clarke has shown very fully why, from his
position as an Englishman, the situation appears to him
in this light. It is scarcely to be expected that it would
appear in any other. Freedom in this liberal sense no
longer exists in countries under a totalitarian régime,
and therefore for them Clarke's conception loses its meaning. It is immaterial whether we deplore this or not. For it
is a fact which must be reckoned with and one which
cannot be reversed. But this does not mean in the least
that the quest for freedom has been extinguished. On the
contrary, the problem of freedom rises once more with
youthful vigour from the immense funeral pyre which has
consumed all the liberal rights of personal and political
freedom, since these rights were considered not only
unnecessary but positively harmful. And now indeed
the problem assumes its original form as the fight for
the freedom of the *Christian* faith and for the freedom
of the Christian conscience. Once the problem is stated
in these terms it is no longer a question of so adjusting
the balance between the freedom of individual action
and development and the necessities and demands of
political and social order as to avoid too great indi-

o

vidualism on the one hand or collectivism on the other, but it becomes a question of what is the highest Court of Appeal binding on man's faith and conscience.

All those engaged in this fight for freedom of conscience and for their Christian faith are convinced that the true depth and meaning of the problem of human freedom is only finally understood when stated in this way. For if the freedom of the individual in political and social life presupposes what a German would describe as a willed acceptance of submission, order, and discipline, and which an Englishman would presumably characterize as common sense, then the problem finally resolves itself into the question: what inner laws must man accept as binding on his faith and conscience if he is to find freedom in obedience and remain obedient while free? This obedience is that imposed by the Christian faith, and this freedom is that found in a Christian life.

A few examples will show the character of this freedom and what it may mean for our present time. As a result of the secularization of the Christian belief in God a number of philosophies came into being, none of which assumed a really dominant position. Scepticism is the hall-mark of our time. This scepticism poses as freedom, but is in reality the opposite of freedom, for in the long run it exposes man to a dreary fatalism ending in many cases in weary resignation and despair, or else resulting in unbridled enthusiasms and the glorification of violence; which in essence are also counsels of despair. Most people are unaware until it is forced upon them by brutal circumstances how close a connection exists between scepticism and violence, and how easily so-called free thought degenerates into tyranny over the faith and conscience of others. In contrast to this, faith in the living God, with whom man enters into personal relationship through prayer, stands for freedom. Yes, this is the freedom on which all true personality is founded since *we* feel ourselves to be persons because He, *God*, has revealed Himself to us as a Person, inasmuch as we believe in the revelation of Himself in the person of Jesus Christ. In classical times men did not have this feeling, nor does the native of India have it to-day, nor do human beings in the mass, as all those will agree who have experienced how easy it is to talk reasonably with individuals, how impossible when dealing with a crowd.

Moreover, our notions of right and wrong, good and bad, true and false have all been blurred and confused by the intellectual chaos of the present day. Scorn is poured on what used to be considered holy, such as marriage and the family, duty and custom, state and Church. Doubt is expressed as to whether it might not be better in certain cases to deprive men forcibly of their lives in the name of pity, or for other reasons of expediency; whether the higher righteousness does not consist in robbing them of their property; whether indeed there is any such thing as a supreme truth to which we owe allegiance, or whether it does not all come down to how cleverly we can tell a lie. This purports to be freedom, for it creates the illusion that man is the measure of all things. But in truth it is the very negation of freedom. This is not obvious while man is still at the stage of criticizing all things, and the consequences of his destructive criticism have not yet come to light. As soon as this happens, however, it becomes abundantly clear that God's Ten Commandments are not merely a human code of ethics which we can accept or reject as we like, but that in very truth God visits the sins of the fathers upon the children unto the third and fourth generation.

We long for fellowship, yet when or where has any true fellowship existed among men unless they recognized that before God no man may boast and that He is no respecter of persons? The most radical "equality" that can possibly exist between men of different races, nationality, class, and sex is that covered by the Christian admission that "we are all sinners one with another." All true social equality presupposes that men should recognize this their fundamental equality before God and express it in their willingness to forgive one another. He who has learnt to forgive is truly free. He who has not yet learnt to do so is still bound. He is bound in *all* the relationships of his life.

Finally, who is truly free who has not achieved liberty face to face with death? This does not mean that one should long for death or hope to find in non-existence an escape from the barrenness and emptiness of an existence which has become unmeaning, for in nothingness there is neither liberty nor bondage, but just precisely nothing. The liberty of which we speak refers to those who have attained a sure faith in the *reality* of the eternal world which began with the risen Christ. "And though they take our life, goods, honour, children, wife, yet is their profit small; these things shall vanish all: the City of God remaineth." This hymn of Luther's is only too often sung by those who know little of the tremendous freedom it expresses.

These considerations must suffice to make clear what is meant by the liberty of the followers of Christ and what such liberty may mean for the present generation. It will perhaps show also what was foreshadowed above, that *all* freedom in political and social life comes as the fruit of this liberty of conscience and belief. This explains why we consider that the educational task of the Church to-day lies in testifying in a clear and unequivocal manner, supported by practice, to the reality of this freedom.

If the Church does this it obviously has nothing to do

with education in the usual meaning of the term. For
education is something given by one person to another,
by one generation to another. The message, however,
which the Church must deliver is no ethical or educational
system of values; it is the revelation of the living God.
With such a gospel to preach, the Church may not
indulge in even the faintest speculation as to whether
"Christianity might not after all be given a trial as a
method of education." But this gospel must be preached
in the firm conviction that it alone represents the one
hope of salvation for mankind, for it alone makes possible
the union between man and the living God. This un-
compromising character of the Christian message will
certainly alienate many people, but, on the other hand,
it is precisely this quality which constitutes its essentially
"educative" power.

On the other hand, it remains true that all really
profound and penetrating thought on the nature of
education, and educational methods when faced with
really serious problems, cannot escape the question as
to what can ultimately exert a binding effect on a man's
belief and conscience. In every critical era this is the
stage at which the old root problems of education and
ethics again make their appearance, problems which have
occupied the great minds of every age. Is there in this
world an Absolute Good, or, as it is more customary
nowadays to put it in educational circles, is there such
a thing as Absolute Value? What is this *one* Good, what
is this highest value, for which mankind shall be educated?
And moreover, does that which we call good stand always
in irreconcilable opposition to what Pestalozzi calls "the
mire of this world"? Thirdly, is there not an irreconcilable antithesis between right thinking and right doing,
between will and achievement?

It would seem to me that these questions are also con-

tained in what Clarke demands of the new type of education which he has in mind. For when he says that it is
of primary importance "to organize and direct the essential process of 'taking on a Culture' by the individual,
a process which is at the same time a development and
enhancement of the individual's own powers," he surely
does not mean that our cultural heritage should be transmitted in its entirety, but only that part of it which is
worth transmitting. But what standards shall we apply
in the choice of good and bad in the cultural heritage
of liberalism? And when Clarke goes on to say that the
second requirement is "to bring about the internalizing
of the ruling sanctions and values of the culture so that,
from being external standards and compulsions they
become consciously accepted and applied as personal
criteria," the question surely resolves itself into just *how*
this can be brought about. Can it and should it be
achieved simply by teaching and custom? But how can
that be done when opinion is so divided as to whether
these fundamental convictions have any *right* to rule, or
whether the truths that some acclaim are not in reality
untruths. How can it be done when a critical attitude
on the part of youth towards the dominant values of a
past civilization is even considered necessary and a sign
of a healthy desire for progress? And thirdly, when Clarke
says the problem is how to train the will so that action
may be in harmony with insight, does not that conceal
the knotty problem of the freedom or unfreedom of the
human will?

The deeper one penetrates into these questions, the
more one feels thrown back on the few basic problems
which lie at the root of all ethics and all educational
systems, problems which were already occupying the
mind of Socrates. Their only solution is to be found in
the gospel of the revelation of the living God in Jesus

Christ. For the root questions which lie at the bottom
of all educational thought are these: What will both bind
and set free the consciences of men? What is the highest
criterion of good and evil, right and wrong, true and
false? Who will release us from guilt? Who will reconcile
us with fate? Who can awaken the power of love without
which there can be no true fellowship? If these questions
remain unanswered, all human education is arrested
midway. But human beings *left to themselves* are quite
unable to answer these questions. Only the gospel of the
revelation of God in Christ can do this. He alone is
absolute Truth, the one true criterion for all decisions
of conscience, who frees us from sin and gives us love.
"Everyone that is of the truth heareth my voice, but
everyone that doeth evil hateth the light, neither cometh
to the light."

If at this stage we hark back once more to what was
said about the present crisis of civilization and the inner
situation of modern man, is it claiming too much to assert
that the modern world resembles a ploughed field waiting
for the seed of the Christian gospel? Do the various
countries really differ so greatly in this respect? Certainly
there exists a difference of degree, inasmuch as in some
countries the inner chaos and lack of faith in the minds
of men has brought them to the brink of ruin, whereas
in others the danger is either not so obvious or has not
gone so far. But the signs of inner disruption are to be
met with everywhere, and as long as the spectre of
another and still more terrible war haunts the minds of
men, so long will they be under the domination of a
universal fear. It is not necessary for the Church to
admonish men with apocalyptic warnings—those dread
images are already present to their minds. The Church
needs to proclaim the peace of God which passes all
understanding.

V. THE EDUCATIONAL TASK OF THE CHURCH AT THE PRESENT TIME

The foregoing will have made apparent the reasons why the educational task of the Church is not conceived as consisting primarily in the Church's influence on the public educational system. As Clarke truly says, educational theory and practice, as embodied in an organized system of education, must always follow the temporary changes taking place in the inner and outer conditions governing society. If civilization becomes more and more secularized, schools will follow suit. It follows that the Church would be hopelessly at the mercy of the various temporary changes due to the spirit of the age, if the fulfilment of her educational duties depended on the machinery of the state or of society. And it is especially unwise for her to rely on the schools. Quite apart from the fact that the attitude of school teachers to the Church is often extremely lukewarm, if not actually inimical, schools are not capable of standing out alone against the forces of disruption manifesting themselves in society. I do not believe that any form of human education is capable of doing this. For in the last resort we are faced with the need for a new spirit among men, and as is well known "the Spirit bloweth where it listeth." It is beyond men's control.

But if it is a fact that our civilization cannot free itself from the Christian tradition even when actuated by anti-Christian motives, and if the present crisis really bears the meaning which we think it does, then if these things are so it becomes more and more obvious that mankind is being prepared for the revelation of the gospel of Christ by the actual experiences of their lives; but this means that their preparation is the work of God Himself. If such is the case, the Church should preach the gospel, believing in the power of the truth with which she has been entrusted, and she should renounce all reliance on propagandist methods and other forms of educational tyranny. The *number* of adherents she gains, or regains, is comparatively unimportant; what does matter is that she should make her meaning clear. Men must feel that this message really affects them in all their troubles whether of mind or circumstance.

The following individual points should be borne in mind:

1. The Church needs a re-statement of Christian truth which shall be in living contact with the questions current in modern thought. She must be willing to learn from the kind of questions asked by modern science, for these are much closer to life than the questions current in traditional theology. That does not mean that she should in any way surrender the truths of faith which she holds in trust. Her task consists rather in pointing out quite clearly once again the dividing line that separates knowing and believing—a division which has been completely obscured in modern thought. Only in this way will the help which theology may give to the natural sciences and which science in its turn may give to the Church become truly mutual. For it is by no means true that science does not need such help. Natural science, as any scientist will admit, is at present undergoing a process of upheaval. The old conception of universal knowledge no longer exists. The intellectual connecting link which bound the various specialized branches of knowledge to each other in a unity has been lost. This becomes all the more painfully obvious when science is confronted with practical tasks involving the lives of human beings. That is why we are beginning to see more clearly wherein lies the cardinal error of former scientific thought. The period of history from which we are just emerging believed in science for the sake of science, a thing which does not

exist, for science is always related to man, and exists for the sake of man, and not man for the sake of science. But if man comes to occupy the central position, the problems of human destiny and guilt, of time and eternity, of the relative and absolute, assume quite another importance. The answer to such questions can no longer be given by knowledge, but only by faith. If knowledge tries to find an answer it becomes transformed into faith. This raises the question: Is this the true faith, is it a faith capable of shouldering such a burden? Once more the limits of reason become apparent. The problem of the *truth* of faith, which cannot be decided on scientific grounds, once more becomes a living question. However impressive the advances of modern science may be—and perhaps they appear most imposing to those who have not quite realized the process of upheaval they are at present undergoing—it must not be supposed that they could ever replace, or even put in the shade, the truths of the Christian faith which belong to quite another category. As soon as scientific theory is put to the test of practice its difficulties immediately become apparent, in psychology no less than in biology.

2. The community needs clear teaching on the root problems of Christian belief. This presupposes sound theology; and the proper fulfilment of this second duty must therefore always go hand in hand with the former. It is a mistake to suppose that the "uneducated" can be fobbed off with half-baked doctrine, or that it is easier to speak to the "masses" than to the "intelligentsia." The opposite is true. The latter can sometimes be humbugged, but the former never in regard to matters touching their practical experience of life. Only the profound is simple, only the simple profound. But this is best learnt by practical experience. Theology which is not put to the practical test of its effect on the com-

munity is, in any case, a thing of no account. This brings
out one of the root evils in the Church. What she says
is partly too complicated and partly directed over the
heads of her hearers. Unprejudiced observation of Church
people of to-day will everywhere reveal the fact that they
lack a knowledge of the elementary truths of the Christian
faith. To begin with, they are ignorant of the Ten
Commandments; still less are they acquainted with the
articles of belief, and their ignorance of Holy Writ is
abysmal. What is required is instruction, instruction, and
once again instruction, and that without any false fear
of so-called intellectualism. For present-day man needs
to be taught *here and now* the meaning of the commandment "thou shalt have none other gods beside me." He
must learn why children should honour their parents;
why it is never right, even for a doctor, to attempt the
life of another; why marriage is holy, etc., and when
all this is placed in a true light and contrasted with the
various confused opinions and misstatements of the
present day, such teaching is not mere intellectualism,
but the living and presumably even the interesting truth.
What is needed is to tell the people these things so clearly
and so incisively that they can recognize the experiences
of their lives in Holy Scripture. That is why it is very
important that the Church of every country should speak
in good, clear, compelling German, English, French,
or whatever other language it may be. For the international journalese, to which man is accustomed at the
present day, spoils his capacity for thought by the use
of superficial phrases, and the most varied assortment
of foreign words, which he only half understands. Many
a matter becomes at once much clearer when it is translated from the phraseology of the newspaper into simple
everyday language such as our forefathers used to express
their thoughts.

3. The mission of the Church must include the cure of souls. This does not mean that the Church should become sentimental or pietistic, but the minister must know the temptations and distresses that afflict modern man and, inspired by the love of Christ, he should be able to speak of these matters in a manner which is both very gentle and yet entirely matter of fact. All true interpretation of Holy Scripture is also an interpretation of the meaning of human life. We have in mind the problems arising from the relations of the sexes, the difficulties of married life, the cares which parents experience in bringing up their children, and especially perhaps the problems of conscience that arise in modern professional life. Added to these are the actual problems of faith with which mankind is faced by destiny, sin, guilt, and death. All these problems should be treated in such a way that those who listen can discern the voice of Christ who is Himself the Truth. In this way they will feel touched in their common humanity, for Christ was very *man* because the love of *God* dwelt in Him.

Obviously this presupposes in the preacher great personal maturity and depth of Christian experience. Not everyone can be expected to have achieved mastery, but everyone must have come in contact with the realities of life in one form or another, and no more is demanded of him than that his testimony should be sincere and frank. Much help can be derived from sound theology. Once the right note has been struck, personal contact between the clergyman and his parishioners usually follows, and under the guidance of the Holy Spirit the good work proceeds. For there is nothing that deepens the theological perceptions and the Christian experience of a clergyman so much as a real concern for the souls of the human beings with whom he associates.

4. It will be needful everywhere to introduce new

habits of Christian behaviour, for habit or custom really means giving an orderly pattern to the events of a day, a year, a whole lifetime. That is absolutely essential. For not only is a world without Christ essentially irreligious, but the same applies to the secularization of time. As is well known, the New Testament uses one and the same word for "world" and "time." A man who lives entirely immersed in the temporal, for whom one day is like another, morning like evening, becomes so obsessed with the endlessness of time that he forgets eternity. Reference might be made here to the significance for the spiritual life of man of the daily habit of reading the newspaper. His mind gets flooded with a multiplicity of temporal happenings, but he loses contact with eternal truth. This is one of the most important symptoms of the worldliness of present-day life. Where formerly you would find the Bible, you now find the daily newspaper, the editor has usurped the place of the priest and the desk that of the pulpit. This fact alone renders possible the centralized control of public opinion as practised to-day in totalitarian states.

Obviously it is not the business of the Church to try to reverse this state of things. The present day and the day's newspaper are not in themselves evil, but they can easily be turned to sinister uses if the Church does not simultaneously lay stress on the *eternal* truth which has been entrusted to her keeping. Moreover, man cannot live merely from day to day and on the day's newspaper articles, and that is why it is the duty of the Church to exhort her followers in all earnestness to the regular hearing of the Word of God. This brings us to the question of keeping holy the Sabbath day, of family prayers, observing Church feasts, and all those matters which link together the passing of time with the outlook on eternity. Do not say that such things are too simple, too primitive.

If the Church is shy of taking these simple primitive things seriously, the rest of the world will not hesitate to act in a still more "primitive" fashion. It is scarcely credible how helpless modern man is, or how easily led if he is approached in the right way, for he has lost the right ordering of his life and his nervousness is largely bound up with the temporal disorder of his existence and the barrier between him and all the forces of eternity.

In this connection we may consider the desirability of forming small groups of people for the discussion of their personal and professional problems. Women especially feel a strong and legitimate desire for such small gatherings, though this need is by no means confined only to women. People in the large cities of to-day have a real longing for neighbourliness and the encouragement resulting from comradeship. But they must actually have something in common which will create a real bond, and the comradeship must have depth and meaning. The Church must attempt to provide an effective counterweight to the type of social gathering now fashionable in which shallow eroticism attempts to mask the absence of real depth of feeling.

All this brings us back to the great question which is of paramount importance for the future of our civilization, namely, whether the Christian Church of the present day still has, or will be given, sufficient inner vitality to create small, living communities from the vast hordes of people living in the great cities of to-day. Success cannot come at once and need not be attained in a hurry, but this is the alpha and omega for the solution of the world crisis of civilization. Until such living communities exist, enshrining one faith and participating in a satisfying community life, the future remains entirely unpredictable, for it is impossible to predict the moods and opinions of the masses. We must therefore reckon with catastrophes, because the masses have a liking for catastrophes. The people will ever run after some new thing, *cupida novarum rerum*, and they know nothing and care less for patience. Their permanent character is change, but not the peace of eternity.

Is the modern Church capable of such an educational task? By her own unaided effort certainly not, but in all that she undertakes she must ever reckon with the help of God. It might seem as if the end could be more rapidly reached by formulating a new educational programme and forcibly imposing it on the people. However that may be, we are brought up against the principle of totalitarianism in education, but nothing can be achieved by hurry. If the universal process of disintegration in society and culture has lasted hundreds of years, it cannot be reversed in ten. The Church needs much humility, much patience, and much love. But she should never doubt that this so-called crisis of civilization is in truth a crisis of faith and can only be properly estimated and dealt with in the light of *that* truth which has been entrusted to her keeping. She must have the certainty of her own indispensability and believe in her own future and in God's promise to her.

VI. THE EUROPEAN EDUCATIONAL PROBLEM AND THE ONE HOLY CHURCH

The cultural and educational crisis with which we are dealing affects the whole of Europe and may even extend beyond its borders. That is why attempts at a political solution are not confined to any one country, but extend in one form or another to all countries. Clarke also seems to hold this view. That is why he says that "the ideal of free personality, just as the closely related ideal of equality, must be looked on as articles of faith of a universal

religion." In parenthesis it may be remarked that the
same claim would presumably also be made for the idea
of a universal communistic world order. This shows how
even here present-day ideas are the heirs of the ideals
of liberalism and humanism, with the characteristic
difference that such a communist world would be set
up by violence and world revolution.

From the standpoint of the Church it may be remarked
that one ideal like the other is an image of the One Holy
Church, *Una Sancta Ecclesia*. It is, therefore, very significant that at a time when the Church is split up into
numerous national churches and sects, the ideal of one
world-embracing community should be reborn in the
world of political thought. So deeply rooted are we in
the traditions of our Christian history.

From the standpoint of spiritual history, the idea of
a League of Nations appears as a secularized version of
the Christian hope in the heavenly kingdom of eternal
peace.[1] Its secularization consists in the fact that a
spiritual hope resting in a universal recognition of Christ
as the Lord of the World, has been transformed into a
political power. But in this form the difficulty of realizing
this ideal in practical life is a constant problem, which,
in the long run, just because we are dealing with political
power, resolves itself into the problem of the collective
use of force. This becomes immediately apparent as soon
as the articles of the League are violated. But all successful use of force would immediately convert the League
of Nations into a Society of Nations, two conceptions
which Kant was careful to keep separate. The attempt
to solve the universal European educational problem by
such an encroachment of the institution of the League
of Nations would necessarily lead to such a Society of
Nations adopting the theory and practise of totalitarianism

[1] Cf. Kant: *Zum ewigen Frieden* (Towards Eternal Peace).

(which hitherto has only been realized by individual nations), and such a situation could only be achieved by completely revolutionizing the world.

The situation appears quite different when a solution to the problems raised by the European educational crisis is sought in the hope that God will bring about closer spiritual union between the Christians of all nations in their common struggle for the truth of their faith and the existence of their Church. The following two instances will show how constantly the feeling after the *Una Sancta* appears in the background of our educational problems : The unity of the "European family of nations" (Ranke) does not consist in their biological and racial relationship nor in the sociological solidarity of the working classes, but it is historically conditioned by their *common Christian tradition*. On this tradition is founded the unity of European culture, nay even the unity of European civilization. However unchristian this civilization may now seem to us, its essentially Christian quality is recognized by non-Christian countries. The greater the national and political strain, the more important it becomes for us to recognize and give shape to the unity of the *Una Sancta Ecclesia* which we possess in the common belief in Christ as our divinely appointed Lord, the Saviour and Judge of all men and of all nations. This is no mere political unity, but its effectiveness and reality depend entirely on how far it becomes a living reality in the spirit of Jesus Christ.

The task which this imposes on us is that in the face of the old and new paganism with which Christians in all countries are faced to-day, we should be fully conscious of what binds us together as *Christians* and what duties are laid upon us as *Christians*.

The second fact which demonstrates clearly the close connection between our educational problems and the *Una*

P

Sancta is shown by the paralysing effect which the multiplicity of sects and their internecine quarrels have on the effectiveness of the Christian gospel. The greater the success achieved in the political sphere by the concentration of political power, the more ridiculous appears the ecclesiastical separatism of the Church of Jesus Christ. Anti-Christian propaganda knows how to use this for its profit, as, for instance, when it directs its attacks not at the religion and rites current at home, but only at those of other countries which are little known to its own peoples and so easily turned to ridicule. In the long run every gibe directed against Christian belief weakens the authority of the Christian Church. That cannot be altered, but it can to some extent be countered by deepening in the consciousness of Christians of all countries their sense of belonging to one universal Christian Church.

Finally, the advent of the *Una Sancta* does not depend on human assent or dissent, but on the measure in which men take up their stand for or against Christ, and on whether the fight which the Church must wage in this or that country is felt to be a matter which concerns Christians of all countries. Only then will men feel each other to be brothers in Christ and will then assist each other as brothers because they will be ceaselessly spurred on by their concern for the honour of their Lord.

SOME CONCLUDING REFLECTIONS

by

J. H. OLDHAM

SOME CONCLUDING REFLECTIONS

THERE is general agreement among the contributors to this volume that there is a crisis in education. The word crisis is often lightly used and may, in consequence, mean little or much. The preceding contributions give to the term a solid substance and impressive weight. Even in America where the outward evidences of a crisis are less obvious than in Europe, Dr. Paul Monroe asserts[1] that very great social changes are in progress, to which education has not yet adjusted itself and that the American educational system, like all others, is facing problems for which a solution has not yet been found and for the treatment of which traditional methods are insufficient. It is, in fact, in the education field that the modern conflict between the Christian and the non-Christian views of life finds many of its most striking manifestations and that the resulting problems in the relations between Church, Community, and State exhibit some of their most characteristic features.

There is a crisis in education because there is a crisis in modern culture, and it is culture—in the sense of the beliefs, standards, and customs prevailing in the community—finding unconscious as well as conscious expression in the school, that is the real educative force. The school is effective, as Professor Clarke has pointed out,[2] only in so far as it concentrates and focuses the educative influences inherent in the prevailing culture, and transmits from generation to generation—often unconsciously even more than by its deliberate and planned organization, curricula, and instruction—the unspoken understandings which give character and meaning to that culture. We are told by some observers that a new type of man is being

[1] P. 81.   [2] Pp. 3, 6, 8, 17.

produced in Russia.[1] But in so far as this is being brought about, it is the result of fundamental changes in the economic and industrial basis of society, and of the consequent new social relations of men with one another, much more than of the conscious efforts of the school. In so far as these have contributed to the change it is because they reflect the new order of society.

The dominant feature of the present situation of which the Church has to take account is the weakening of the hold on men's minds of the Christian understanding of life and consequently the break-down of the ethos inspired by it and the culture of which it was one of the main determinants. In wide areas the essential Christian affirmations are openly repudiated. Elsewhere, there is an inner decay of their influence. For growing numbers they have ceased to have a living meaning. The process has gone much further in some countries than in others. It is those in which its advance has been greatest that are instructive for all. What has taken place there opens our eyes to realities which are often concealed by the continued nominal adherence of large numbers to the Christian tradition and by the lingering power of entrenched custom and traditional prestige.

The differences in different countries are wide and important. But they should not blind us to the underlying similarities which are perhaps deeper and more significant than the differences. Everywhere the State or the community is tending to establish education on new foundations and to adopt new aims and methods. Everywhere large sections of the younger generation are distrustful of all tradition and desirous of striking out on new paths. Everywhere the Church is being pushed to the circumference of men's lives and interests. If an open conflict is

[1] Cf. Thomas L. Harris, *Unholy Pilgrimage* (Round Table Press, New York).

avoided it is often because the Church has itself become secularized and offers little resistance to prevailing tendencies. The consequences of this crisis in men's ultimate beliefs—which one of the contributors rightly describes as in essence a crisis of *faith*[1]—are plainly set forth in the preceding pages. The cement which holds society together is the general acceptance of certain common assumptions, expressed or implied, in its relations, activities and institutions, as to what is good and what is bad, what is just and what is unjust, what is permissible and what is forbidden. Where such acceptance is lacking society must fall to pieces. In some countries the process of disintegration has proceeded so far that these common presuppositions no longer exist. The State is driven in consequence to an energetic attempt to provide a new basis of social order. The essential fact, as Professor Clarke reminds us,[2] is the social and cultural break-down itself, rather than the philosophy which attempts to repair it. In seeking for such a philosophy, the State may be forced to recognize that it cannot restore unity to the common life on the basis of Christian beliefs and values, since these have entirely lost their hold on large sections of the population. It therefore feels itself driven to discover or create some "myth" to be the centre of national unity. It attempts to establish what is in effect a new religion, and where this course is embarked on the conflict with the Church becomes inevitable, since its understanding of life is an obstacle to the spread of the new faith.

The position of the Church where ideas of liberty and toleration prevail is outwardly much more favourable. But the experience of the Church where it has to contend with totalitarian tendencies compels us to ask whether all is as well under a liberal system as we have been accustomed to suppose, and whether the Christian faith has not

[1] Pp. 177–8, 192.   [2] P. 9.

been exposed in an era of toleration to insidious dangers which we have failed sufficiently to recognize. As the writer of the anonymous contribution in this volume points out,[1] Christianity under a liberal regime comes to be regarded as merely *one* among many possible conceptions of life and of the world, and this attitude insensibly and fatally undermines the Christian claim that Christ is the sole Lord of life and that in Him alone is salvation to be found. It is a mistake to regard the position of the Church under a liberal system as normal. The condition of the Church conforms much more closely to New Testament standards when it finds itself in conflict with a claim on the part of the State to absolute authority that is irreconcilable with the ultimate loyalty of the Church to God alone.

The same danger of the surreptitious sapping of the foundations of the Christian faith by the all-pervading influence of a secular culture is the theme of Mr. Smith's paper. It is possible for Christianity to be tolerated and even accorded public recognition and given an acknowledged place in the school and yet for the effect of the teaching to be overborne and over-weighted by the insistent pressure of the secular assumptions prevalent in the society, the life of which is reflected in the school.

Mr. Morris sees, and states very clearly, the educational problem in countries with a liberal tradition. Education could afford to concern itself in the main with the intellect "so long as the general direction of a man's life could be taken for granted." But in a world in which "there is no strong current of religious, moral, social, or political orthodoxy" the problem of education assumes a very different shape. The task of the educator under these conditions is to help men to find a cause to which they can freely devote themselves. Only through such self-devotion

[1] P. 184.

can there come the vigour which finds expression in new energies and bends life to new purposes. Human life finds its fulfilment, as multitudes of adherents of the new movements are discovering to-day, not in an unfettered choice between endless possibilities but in the dedication of the whole self to the service of a commanding end.

The crucial problem confronting education is the question of freedom and authority. It is on this point that the contributions to this volume lay the strongest emphasis. As one of them says,[1] "the problem of freedom is the root problem of all education." The same writer shows how this problem of freedom must of necessity present itself in different forms in democratic and in totalitarian countries. It is by exposing our minds to this sharp and deep contrast that we may perhaps best arrive at the true meaning of Christian freedom.

Professor Clarke takes as his starting-point the growth of free personality as the goal of education. This ideal has the power, as he truly says, to evoke the passionate enthusiasm of teachers, not only in England, but in democratic countries generally, and it lies at the heart of the humanistic conception of education which from the time of the Renaissance has tended more and more to dominate education in Europe. The individual is set over against the world, and his task is to understand it, to appropriate it, and to master it. The movement, as Professor Zenkowsky points out,[2] was a right and necessary assertion of freedom against the restrictions placed by the Church on thought and inquiry and against its tendency to engulf the personality. It opened up lines of progress which can never be retraced. The gains of this breaking of all fetters which confined the human spirit are unquestionable and splendid. The humanistic ideal of the all-round personality has found expression in individual lives of brilliant

[1] P. 192. [2] Pp. 37–8.

richness. It has been education, as Mr. Morris says, "after
the grand manner."

But there is a reverse side to the picture. Great as have
been the achievements of the humanistic ideal, its effects
in other directions have been disastrous. Because the
possibilities are endless on every side life tends to lack
direction and clearness of aim. Hence, the result is apt to
be that lack of "vigour" which Mr. Morris deplores. As
Professor Tillich has pointed out,[1] the defect of this conception of education is that while everything is interesting,
nothing makes an unconditional demand. There is no
unconditional claim to give to life meaning and direction.
Moreover, this type of education is the privilege of a few
individuals or of a class. The masses are of necessity
excluded from it. It is fundamentally individualistic and
cannot create community. It leaves unsolved the problems
to which Professor Clarke, Mr. Morris, and other contributors to this volume so forcibly direct attention. How is
freedom to be prevented from developing into licence and
self-seeking egoism, and so proving destructive of all
community? Where are we to find the sources of social
obligation? How in education is provision to be made for
discipline?

One of the most radical criticisms of humanistic education is found in the writings of Professor Eberhard Grisebach.[2] The world of humanism he regards as an unreal
world because it has its centre in the self. Co-operation
between individuals is indeed indispensable in scientific
and humanistic studies. But the necessity arises solely from
the limitation of the individual's powers. The barriers are
not in principle insurmountable. In the last resort it is the
individual who chooses what he will assimilate and what
he will reject. Nowhere in this field does the self encounter

[1] *Religiöse Verwirklichung*, p. 183.

[2] *Gegenwart*, 1928; *Freiheit und Zucht*, 1936.

an irremovable barrier. Nowhere does it meet a reality which effectively limits it and which it is wholly outside its power to change or control. The inescapably real is met with only when the self encounters another self—when a person meets another person having his own similar, unique, and independent centre of life. Here the self in its infinite expansion meets with a real limitation. Here we experience contradiction. A demand is made on us to which we must respond. Here in this encounter in the living present, in contrast with the world of memory, we find ourselves face to face with stern, inescapable reality. We are no longer free to choose, to judge, to assimilate, as we will. At this point our freedom encounters a limit. We are called upon to respond to a demand which is not within our own control but which comes to us from without. We have to submit to the tension, to endure the contradiction, to suffer. It is these experiences of the encounter of person with person, of the clash of will with will, that constitute real education. Yet little regard, or none at all, is paid to them in a humanistic education.

We are thus led to the fundamental question of the nature of community. Too often the attempt has been made to take the individual as a self-subsisting entity and to inquire how he can be brought into harmonious relations with other individuals. But the isolated individual is an abstraction. We exist as persons only in relation with other persons. Many, again, would look for unity in a common outlook, in the acceptance of a common world-view, in the cherishing of common ideals, and in devotion to common ends. These undoubtedly create genuine bonds, but the question may be raised whether they do not at the same time beget illusory hopes in so far as they leave out of the reckoning the profound differences which exist between men—the radical "otherness" of the other just because he is other. True community, Professor

Grisebach would maintain, is realized not in eliminating the differences or in attempting to bring others into agreement with one's own view—to succeed in which would be to create an individual, solitary world—but in the endurance of the contradiction and the joyful acceptance of the continuous tension between two opposed points of view, each of which renounces the claim to be absolute.

The ultimate ground and guarantee of free personality against the engulfing claims of the State or of the community is, as Professor Clarke says,[1] religious. The denial of freedom in totalitarian states is compelling Christians to seek for a deeper understanding of the meaning of Christian freedom. Under these conditions, as the writer of the preceding paper says,[2] "the problem of freedom rises once more with youthful vigour from the immense funeral pyre which has consumed all the liberal rights of personal and political freedom." This paper contains an impressive description of the nature of Christian freedom. It is an inner freedom. Essentially it is a freedom from self—from egocentricity. This is a deliverance greater than deliverance from outward fetters. It can be brought about only from without. Only a love which meets us from outside can free us from our self-centredness. Henceforward, the centre of our lives is no longer in ourselves but in the one who loves us. Christian freedom is the freedom of those who have been forgiven and who have the power to forgive. It is the freedom of those who have been delivered from the fear of death, which is man's last enemy. It is the freedom of those who know themselves to be the sons of God, and who in the power of that relationship are triumphant over evil and over circumstances. It is a freedom which is realized in the joyous service of God and for His sake in the service of men. It consists in the glad acceptance of the obligation to seek the good of

[1] Pp. 21–2.   [2] P. 193.

other men as the means of realizing the highest freedom in and through the relation with other persons. It is revealed, as Professor Zenkowsky says,[1] "not in the isolation of human beings from each other, but in a brotherly union of all in Christ." While it is rooted in the profound depths of personality, "it is not given to the isolated individual, but to the many in mystical union through brotherly love; in other words, it is given to the Church."

The supreme task of the Church is to testify to this freedom and to manifest it in the lives of its members. The Church knows that no external measures can ever bind men's consciences or make them inwardly free. Man's freedom is freedom to choose and to realize the good, and that is something that no compulsion or propaganda or instruction can achieve. It can only come about through an inward change. This truth is central in Christ's teaching. *Make the tree good.*

This inner freedom is, and has been in history, the source of social and political liberties. Since it is freedom to serve and obey God it must prompt to actions which bring those who possess it and act on it into conflict with tyrannical restrictions of the human spirit. Where and how the issue must be joined are questions which the individual conscience has to decide in concrete situations. But the first task of Christians is to recover and realize the inner freedom which is the source and spring of all other liberties.

Christians ought, therefore, to be able to perceive clearly the deceptiveness and inadequacy of the proposed remedies for the disease of the modern world and of current endeavours to re-create the bonds which unite men with one another in a genuine fellowship. They do not offer men, as Professor Zenkowsky points out,[2] a genuine and complete freedom in which they can meet the demands of life in its wholeness but only a restricted and fettered

[1] P. 37.   [2] Pp. 42–3, 59–60.

freedom within the limits of a particular scheme of life imposed from above. Those who look to these solutions tend, as Mr. Morris shows,[1] to have recourse to propaganda and the arts of mass suggestion rather than to concern themselves with the disinterested education of the whole personality. Nor, as the writer of the last of the papers reminds us,[2] are these measures, which are directed primarily to political ends, capable of meeting the more fundamental human needs of the individual person in his hopes and fears, frustrations and anxieties, in his quest for a satisfying meaning of life and in facing the inevitable end of his mortal existence. Moreover, if an intense loyalty to the nation has the power to subordinate individual self-seeking to the common good, an extreme nationalism only transfers the anarchy of individualism to the international sphere by setting nation against nation, each remaining a law to itself. The Christian, therefore, while recognizing much that is good and salutary and necessary in the endeavours to arrest the disintegration of society, will none the less perceive clearly the inadequacy of the means to achieve the desired end. He will not be content complacently to criticize these efforts, but, seeing that the need is desperate, will be impelled to think out what are the true remedies in order that he may be prepared when disillusionment comes, as come it must, to direct men's minds to their real hope of salvation.

Christians must at the same time recognize that the new movements are justified in their revolt against a selfish individualism which must end inevitably in the dissolution of society. Community cannot be found in the attempt to reconcile the arbitrary desires and caprices of a multitude of separate individuals. Unity can be found only in the devotion of the individual to an end beyond himself. Men are turning to-day from the burden of an unchartered

[1] P. 93.   [2] P. 188.

freedom and the quicksands of their own unfettered choices to seek satisfaction in some reality outside themselves. The Marxist asks men to surrender themselves to the realization of the classless society which the forces of history are inexorably bringing about. The national-socialist claims their whole-hearted devotion to the national community in its wholeness and to the historic soul which inspires its life. What is the objective reality which for the Christian has a superior claim to any of these? It must be something other than a subjective ideal. Our own conceptions of what is right and desirable cannot bind or command us. If our ideals are of our own choosing, since we have chosen them, we can by a change of mind, or under the pressure of fear or inconvenience, abandon them. Only something outside our own control can bind us. Only in the dedication of ourselves to a reality which meets and challenges us can we find the true fulfilment of our lives and the "vigour" which comes from being at the disposal of a Power not ourselves which we can absolutely trust. The Christian confession, as Professor Kohnstamm reminds us, is *Kurios Christus*. The vital question for mankind is, in the phrase of Professor Tillich, whether history has a centre—whether there exists a central reality which gives to the historical life of men a commanding meaning. To the various competing ends to which men surrender themselves Christian faith opposes the supreme, decisive reality of the love of God revealed in Jesus Christ. It maintains, that is to say, that the ultimate reality in human life is personal fellowship, rooted in God's love for men, and that human life finds its meaning and fulfilment in relations of love and service.

It is only in the relationship of love that the problem of the individual and the community can find its solution. Where love is lacking, the individual must be sacrificed to the community or the community to the individual. We must end either in an anarchic individualism or in the totalitarian state. Only in the free and glad surrender of the self to a God who loves us and whom we love in return with our whole hearts, and whose service is consequently perfect freedom, is a solution found of the problem of freedom and authority.

The great task of the Church is to recall men's minds to the true meaning of freedom and the true basis of community. This cannot be done by preaching alone. The nature of love is such that it must be incarnated in life. To be understood, it must be exhibited, not merely described or affirmed. Christianity has retained its hold on men's minds through successive generations because they have seen it exemplified in lives of convincing quality and attractive beauty. In the fellowship of the Christian community they have found forgiveness, redemption, sympathy, support, and renewed hope. All this has been obscured through the intellectualization of Christianity of which Professor Kohnstamm writes.[1] In order that Christian instruction might find a place in the school curriculum— itself conceived too often in almost exclusively intellectual terms—Christianity has been reduced to something that can be taught. There are things about Christianity which can be taught, but not its essence and soul. Its true nature is disastrously misunderstood when it is thought of primarily as a body of facts and doctrines requiring intellectual assent. If the task of Christian education is to be taken in hand afresh it must be with the determination to present the Christian faith and life in its fulness and not merely an intellectual account of it.

Where the reality of community has been lost, the task of recovering it must begin in small groups. In an arresting passage the writer of the anonymous paper in this volume points out that for multitudes of people to-day the world

[1] Pp. 145–6.

has become a frightening place, because love has departed from it. The question of paramount importance, therefore, for the future of civilization is whether the Church to-day possesses the inner vitality to create small communities possessing a genuine social life, bound together in mutual support and service, and dedicated to promoting the good of the community as a whole. Such groups would be the living germs of a new social consciousness and the creators of a true community life.[1]

What is fundamentally at stake in the modern world is our understanding of the nature and destiny of man. Underlying the policies of Church, Community, and State in education is the conception which each entertains at any given time of the meaning of man's life. This is the ultimate, though by no means always the actual, issue in the historical conflicts which arise. In some instances the controversy may be no more than a struggle between institutions for the control of schools. But in proportion as those concerned with education reflect deeply on their aims, the question: What is man? cannot be evaded. There is no question on the answer to which the future of mankind more depends than on the question whether we believe that man is merely the plaything of blind natural forces, or that he is himself the source of all values in the world, or, on the other hand, that he has been created to become a free son of God.

This fundamental issue whether man is made for time or for eternity is the theme of Mr. Smith's paper. The point which he seeks to drive home is that Christian faith clings to the one view while the society of which the school is a part and the life for which it prepares its pupils are based on quite other assumptions. Here lies an irrecon-

---

[1] Pp. 183, 206. From a different point of view the same idea finds powerful literary expression in Mr. Middleton Murry's *The Necessity of Pacifism*.

cilable conflict, the effects of which may be all the more disastrous because the conflict is latent and not explicit and open. The situation is clearer in the mission field where the distinctive Christian view of life is in marked contrast with the surrounding environment. Similarly, the powerful anti-Christian movements of our time are making plain the radical nature of the issues. Those who live in countries where Christianity is tolerated and a liberal tradition persists have need to open their eyes to what is happening in the world as a whole. The events of our time are making manifest that what is at stake is the relation of the Christian understanding of life to the prevailing attitudes and practices of a secular and largely pagan society.

The unavoidable conflict between these sharply opposed views of man in modern society, and consequently in public systems of education, compels us to consider the relation of Christian faith to the general task of education. There are those who would say, categorically, that the two are totally unrelated. They would maintain that the Church has nothing to do with education in the usual meaning of the term. This point of view directs attention to a profound truth. The act of faith is something *sui generis*. To hear and respond to God's unconditional demand is to be brought into a new dimension—to use a term the far-reaching significance of which has been impressively brought out by Professor Karl Heim.[1] The awakening of faith is God's act alone. It is not something that human effort or skill can ever bring about.

But this vital truth does not imply that the Church can be indifferent to the influences which are brought to bear on the growing child. It is a matter of common experience that the physical and the spiritual are intimately related. Certain bodily states are inimical to moral and spiritual

[1] *The Transcendent God* (Nisbet).

growth. Cretinism is an extreme example. If this is true, there is no reason why it should not be equally true that faults in training, and more particularly in the training of the emotions, may have the effect of closing the mind to the religious appeal or of bringing it about that if that appeal should be heard the response finds expression in base and perverted forms. Emotional biases may be created which dull the conscience completely to the voice of God or lead to grave misinterpretations of its meaning. Because of the indissoluble unity of the human person the Church must both hold unwaveringly to the truth that the Gospel is something that is beyond human control and, hence, outside educational processes, and at the same time be profoundly and actively interested in those processes, lest they interpose insuperable hindrances to the understanding and receiving of the Gospel.

In the task of Christian education, which is the specific responsibility of the Church, our concern cannot be with anything less than the whole man. To take in hand this task, as it ought to be taken in hand, in the full light of modern knowledge will necessitate far-reaching changes in the forms of Christian ministry. The supreme task of the Church must always be to proclaim the Divine Word. But we miss the heart of the matter when, yielding to the subtle pressure of the methods of preaching and instruction on which we chiefly rely, we intellectualize the Gospel. The Gospel entrusted to us is a message of salvation. We are always in danger of accepting as substitutes for salvation two things, more easily attained, which are not salvation. The one is doctrinal belief, and the other is the habit of attendance at religious services. If a person professes the right doctrine and is diligent in attendance at church we take this as evidence that he is a Christian. But a man may do both these things and yet remain hard, grasping, uncharitable, censorious, a detractor of others.

and entirely self-centred. Salvation means emancipation from fear, deliverance from egotism and ego-centricity, and the joyous service of God and of men in the freedom of sonship.

Such freedom, as we have seen, can only be found in a living relation to a loving personal God. But just as Christ devoted His ministry to the healing of men's bodies as well as their souls, so the Church must not only proclaim the Word which makes men free, but also in the fulness of its love for men direct its ministries to removing these infirmities of body, mind, and spirit which are barriers to the reception of that Word. The Christian education of the young is not merely, or even primarily, a matter of instruction, but the communication of a vital experience of personal relationship and community. It must, no less than general education, take account of the different phases in the growth of the individual, of the variety of types of individual and of the ways in which the growing person is at different ages affected by his environment. The effective fulfilment of the Christian ministry requires not only a growing appreciation on the part of Christian preachers and teachers of the scientific understanding of man, but practical co-operation, where it can be brought about, between ministers of the Gospel and doctors, psychiatrists, social welfare workers, and school teachers.

We are thus brought to consider, finally, the relation of the Church to public education. This is often treated as though it were the central issue. It is evident, however, that in many countries Christian teaching, and even all Christian influence, is deliberately excluded from the schools. In countries in which Christian schools, or Christian teaching in schools maintained by the public authority, are still permitted, the fullest advantage should be taken of the opportunity so long as it lasts. The inclusion

of Christian teaching in the system of public education
has the great advantage—among others—of disseminating
among the general population a knowledge of the facts,
history, and doctrines of Christianity. This is a gain, even
when the knowledge is in the main merely intellectual.

It is important, however, to take a realistic view, and
not to exaggerate the importance either of Church schools
or of Christian instruction in public schools. The difference
between Church schools and State schools is often less than
we suppose. We allow ourselves to be misled by the fact
that in the curriculum of the former a place is provided for
Christian instruction. If it is true, however, as was
asserted at the beginning of this paper, that the real
educative influence is that of the prevailing culture transmitted through the school, this force will operate in both
Church schools and State schools, and the power of a
religious lesson to counteract its influence may easily be
exaggerated. Moreover, we shall do well to ponder the
arresting statement in the paper by Mr. Morris[1] that Church
schools in England do not, at the present time, represent or
express the really vital differences in modern society. In
the profound struggle regarding ultimate beliefs, which is
taking place in the world to-day, Christianity can have no
important future unless it stands for something distinctive,
challenging, and supremely significant.

Where it is possible to establish and conduct a Christian
school which attempts to give expression to a genuine
Christian understanding of life in all its aspects, in contrast with the assumptions and practices of a secular or
pagan society, it is essential that the staff should be convinced Christians, whole-heartedly committed to the
Christian way of life. The fundamental problem is that of
the teachers. The best examples of efforts of this kind are
perhaps found in the mission field. In the best of the

[1] Pp. 107–8.

Christian educational institutions in non-Christian countries there is a staff of enthusiastic Christian teachers striving in common to make of the school a Christian society, the life of which offers a marked contrast to that of society in general. But where the sharp distinction between the Christian and the secular life has become blurred, there may be little difference between Church schools and State schools in the extent to which they reflect the prevailing ideas and habits of society, and the religious teaching in the former may be little more than the presentation of an intellectual set of beliefs which involve no fundamental change of life.

Where the opportunity is given of establishing a Christian school which aims at realizing in all its activities the ends of a Christian society, there is every reason for taking advantage of it. That variations from the prevailing type of schools are advantageous even in the national interest is an argument which may in favourable circumstances win the assent even of those who are not themselves Christians. Variety of educational experiment provides an opportunity for conceptions and ways of life which are temporarily undervalued, but which may, none the less, contain the seeds of promise for the future, to make their contribution to the national life. It is not to be expected, however, that those who are committed to the endeavour to create national unity through the schools will readily accept this view, and opportunities for whole-hearted experiments in Christian education are in the present state of the world likely to be rare.

We have witnessed in recent years widespread attempts in certain countries to use the schools as a means of imposing a particular doctrine and philosophy of life on the entire population. In view of these dangers there is strong reason to insist that the proper task of the school is to render to society a technical and specialized service. Its primary business is to impart the knowledge, insight, and skill that are demanded by social necessity, that must be acquired in youth, and that call for skilled guidance and instruction in their acquisition. The facts mentioned in Professor Zenkowsky's paper are of extreme interest in this connexion.[1] The schools in Russia, he tells us, have now been freed from their political objectives. The task of forming a new type of human being and of cultivating enthusiasm for the communist view of life has been transferred from the schools to the youth organizations. The former are permitted to limit themselves to their more strictly educational objectives. Similarly in Italy the effort to capture the soul of youth is actively pursued in youth organizations rather than in the schools. Mr. Morris, again, evidently looks more to adult education than to the schools as the field in which the free association committed to the realization of specific purposes, which he desiderates, may most successfully be developed.[2]

The view that the school, like other specialized activities in the community, has its own distinctive technical function to perform, implies a more modest estimate of the services which schools can render to the nation than the expectations which sometimes find expression in enthusiastic gatherings of teachers. Christian teachers in particular, in proportion to the fervour of their conviction, may be reluctant to accept a view which would appear to limit the opportunities and possibilities of the school. The question may be asked, however, whether it is not necessary and important to distinguish more clearly than we are accustomed to do between the responsibilites of the Christian teacher as a person and his responsibilities as a teacher.

The teacher, like the doctor, the lawyer, the farmer, and the engineer, has his own distinctive vocation and his

[1] Pp. 49–50, 56.   [2] Pp. 111–12, 117.

specialized contribution to make to the life of the community. He is not in his professional capacity concerned with reforming the world. Propaganda lies outside his sphere. His first duty as a Christian teacher is to discharge with faithfulness and thoroughness the particular task assigned to him.

On the other hand it belongs to the nature of his calling that, in contrast with the farmer, whose main concern is with the soil and what it grows, or the engineer, who works with material things, he is engaged all the time with persons. He is concerned, moreover, with persons at the formative period in their growth. In a boarding-school in particular he fills in some measure the place of the absent parents. As a Christian, he must recognize his responsibility to all other persons with whom he is brought into contact. In his relations with his pupils he thus has inescapable responsibilities as a person in addition to those which he has as teacher.

The Christian teacher cannot, of course, divide himself into two separate halves. The unity of his personality must express itself in all his acts. He cannot discard his ultimate beliefs or refuse to allow them to determine all his judgments and attitudes. It is his duty as a Christian to bear fearless witness to his faith by his acts and, where occasion requires, also by his words. It is possible, however, to distinguish these Christian responsibilities from the carrying out of his professional task in accordance with its own specific, technical requirements. The extent to which these two sets of responsibilities may in practice coincide depends on circumstances. In a school which is known to be a Christian school, and to which pupils are sent on that understanding, it is possible for all the activities of the school to be unified in a single dominating purpose. At the other extreme a Christian may be a teacher in a school in which any explicit teaching or overt Christian influence would be resented by the authorities or by the parents of the pupils, and the teacher has in consequence to restrict himself in the school to the fulfilment of his professional duties. The resulting tension between his responsibilities as a Christian and as a teacher is similar to that involved in every attempt to live as a Christian in an un-Christian or incompletely Christian society.

This paper, like the others in the volume, has had to be confined to a consideration of principles. A discussion of their application is impossible, since the conditions in different countries are widely different, and since the field of education includes an immense variety of tasks and responsibilities, e.g. those of parents, of the clergy, of teachers in various grades of schools, and of those concerned with the control and administration of education. To discuss in the concrete these quite distinct responsibilities is outside the scope of the present paper. Moreover, the Church is confronted to-day with a fundamentally new situation in which the experience of the past no longer affords sufficient guidance. This volume will have achieved its purpose if it succeeds in bringing that fact home and planting it deeply in the minds of its readers.

The problems to which attention has been directed call for much further study and constructive thought by those who have the equipment and leisure to undertake it. As Mr. Smith has pointed out,[1] there is an urgent need for the working out on fresh lines of a Christian theology and Christian ethic related to the needs and tasks of the present day. It is no less important that individuals and groups should set to work where they are, and ask themselves what their Christian faith demands in the circumstances in which they have to live and act. What is wanted more than anything else is a rapidly increasing number of "cells," or small groups of people who are feeling their

[1] Pp. 131-2, cf. pp. 201-2.

way to the discovery of the Christian witness and action
that are called for in the present state of society. It is to a
multitude of such experiments, prompted and guided by
the Holy Spirit, and undertaken in the spirit of Christian
adventure and in a deep and growing awareness of the
realities of the present crisis, that we must look for a
vitalizing and renewal of the life of the Church.

OVERLEAF

particulars of publications
of similar interest
issued by

GEORGE ALLEN & UNWIN LTD
LONDON: 40 MUSEUM STREET, W.C.1
LEIPZIG: (F. VOLCKMAR) HOSPITALSTR. 10
CAPE TOWN: 73 ST. GEORGE'S STREET
TORONTO: 91 WELLINGTON STREET, WEST
BOMBAY: 15 GRAHAM ROAD, BALLARD ESTATE
WELLINGTON, N.Z.: 8 KINGS CRESCENT, LOWER HUTT
SYDNEY, N.S.W.: AUSTRALIA HOUSE, WYNYARD SQUARE

Philosophical Bases of Theism

by G. DAWES HICKS. "The most valuable feature of the work is the fact that its quiet and reasoned argument leads up to a vigorous refutation of pantheism, alike on philosophic and on religious grounds . . . this book contains a particularly careful and discriminating criticism of positivism and . . . of its modern form."— EVELYN UNDERHILL in *Spectator*. *Hibbert Lectures*.

Demy 8vo. 8s. 6d.

Religion in its Essence and Manifestation

by G. VAN DER LEEUW. Translated by J. E. Turner. This book is not meant as a "History of Religion," but it seeks to penetrate beyond the facts to the underlying mental attitude. The book, which is imbued with an original and inquisitive spirit, deals with God and the Divine; Man in his religious attitude; and with the chief types of religion and religious personality.

Small Royal 8vo. 25s.

Germany's New Religion

by WILHELM HAUER, KARL HEIN, KARL ADAM. Translated by T. S. K. Scott-Craig and R. E. Davies. "This interesting volume sets side by side an account of the German Faith Movement and two refutations, one by a leading Protestant, the other by an eminent Roman Catholic."—*Times Literary Supplement*.

"The book is one of intense interest which everyone who wants to keep in touch with the religious movements in Germany should read."—*Manchester Guardian*.

"This book gives the reader a clear idea of the conflict of faiths which is taking place in Germany, the storm-centre of religion at the present time."—*Scotsman*.

All prices are net. *Cr. 8vo. 5s.*

LONDON: GEORGE ALLEN & UNWIN LTD